DO WE NEED A COHABITATION AGREEMENT?

DO WE NEED A COHABITATION AGREEMENT?

UNDERSTANDING HOW A LEGAL CONTRACT CAN STRENGTHEN YOUR LIFE TOGETHER

MICHAEL G. COCHRANE

B.A. LL.B.

John Wiley & Sons Canada, Ltd.

Library and Archives Canada Cataloguing in Publication Data

Cochrane, Michael G. (Michael George), 1953-
Do we need a cohabitation agreement? : understanding how a legal contract can strengthen your life together / Michael G. Cochrane.

Includes index.
ISBN 978-0-470-73750-7

1. Cohabitation agreements—Canada—Popular works. 2. Unmarried couples—Legal status, laws, etc—Canada—Popular works. 3. Common-law marriage—Canada—Popular works. I. Title.

KE590.C62 2010 346.7101'6 C2010-900205-9
KF538.C62 2010

Production Credits
Cover design: Adrian So
Cover photo credit: ©Getty/Photodisc/Ross Anania
Interior text design and typesetter: Natalia Burobina
Printer: Printcrafters Inc.

John Wiley & Sons Canada, Ltd.
6045 Freemont Blvd.
Mississauga, Ontario L5R 4J3

Printed in Canada

1 2 3 4 5 PC 14 13 12 11 10

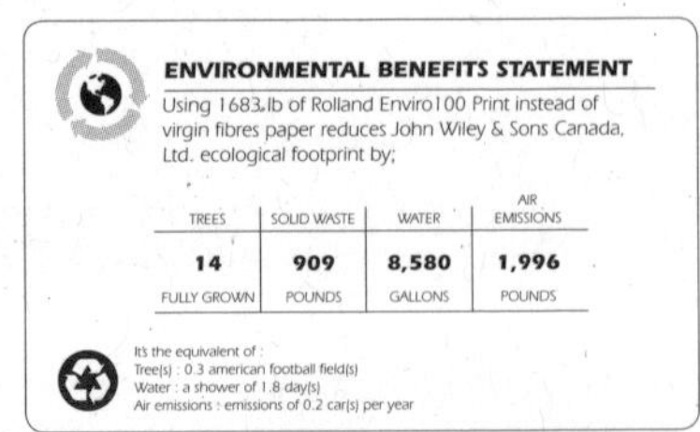

ENVIRONMENTAL BENEFITS STATEMENT

Using 1683 lb of Rolland Enviro100 Print instead of virgin fibres paper reduces John Wiley & Sons Canada, Ltd. ecological footprint by;

TREES	SOLID WASTE	WATER	AIR EMISSIONS
14	**909**	**8,580**	**1,996**
FULLY GROWN	POUNDS	GALLONS	POUNDS

It's the equivalent of :
Tree(s) : 0.3 american football field(s)
Water : a shower of 1.8 day(s)
Air emissions : emissions of 0.2 car(s) per year

CONTENTS

ACKNOWLEDGEMENTS

I would like to acknowledge a few important people and their contribution to this book. The first person is Rosa Becker. In this book, you will learn more about her and her experiences in the Canadian justice system as a common-law spouse. She killed herself in 1986 in a hopeless protest over her treatment as a common-law spouse who fought for her rights all the way to the Supreme Court of Canada. I hope that a book like this educates Canadians so that there will be no more Rosa Beckers.

I would like to acknowledge also the combined forces of my literary agent, Daphne Hart, of Helen Heller agency (www.helenhelleragency.com) and my publisher, John Wiley & Sons Canada Ltd., who have worked with me as an author for this series of books about family law in Canada. This book, as well as *Surviving Your Divorce: A Guide to Canadian Family Law* and *Do We Need a Marriage Contract?: Understanding How a Legal Agreement Can Strengthen Your Life Together*, is all about educating Canadians to be able to help themselves and to know when they need the help of professionals.

My assistant, Lisa Henry, deserves special mention as she is the one who helped me transform my scribbles into a manuscript over some very long days and nights.

Who we pick as our partners in life is critical to our happiness and I hope that as my daughters, Emma, Erica, Renée, and Hanna, head off into the world and form their important relationships, they take some of my advice to heart. If any of them were about to live common law I would be sure to sit them down and hand them this book. Thanks too to my wife, Rita, who has shown great patience as I disappear for extended periods to do my writing. Thanks, Love.

Michael Cochrane
Partner, Ricketts, Harris LLP
181 University Avenue, Suite 816
Toronto, Ontario M5H 2X7

mcochrane@rickettsharris.com
www.rickettsharris.com
www.michaelcochrane.ca

CAUTION ABOUT LEGAL INFORMATION

The purpose of this book is to help Canadians who are living in common law relationships or who are thinking about living with someone without getting married. I am providing legal information in this book, not legal advice. To obtain legal advice about the way that this information may apply to or affect your personal situation, I recommend that you speak with an experienced family law lawyer in your province or territory. This book is designed to make the conversation easier, less expensive, and more helpful.

1

IS THIS BOOK FOR YOU?

As I prepared the final manuscript for this book and did some last-minute updating of my legal research, a very interesting court case involving a common-law couple in Ontario was published in the law journals. The case is interesting because it provides so many insights into the legal and emotional challenges faced by common-law couples if their relationship does not work out and they separate. I thought, as I read the case (which contains some frightening aspects), that it was a perfect example of what I want Canadians to avoid. This situation should not have happened, but it did. The legal fighting took six years to make its way through our courts (one year longer than the couple actually lived together) and it cost the couple hundreds of thousands of dollars in legal fees. Here is what happened.

A REAL—AND REVEALING—CASE

Ms. Tracy McLean and Mr. Darko Danicic began dating in the summer of 1998, and by September he had given her an engagement ring that had once been his mother's. By Christmas they had moved in together, living in and renovating a property that Darko had purchased before they met. They lived together for five years, from 1998 to 2003. In addition to the house that they lived in, Mr. Danicic bought an empty lot in 2000. The pair worked like pioneers to clear land and build a cottage on it. Then, interestingly, both properties were registered in the name of Mr. Danicic alone. While Ms. McLean worked and put every penny of her $55,000 per year salary into running their household, Mr. Danicic ran a photography business. She helped him with the business as well as running the household, including the cooking, cleaning, and grocery shopping. You name it, she did it. And she worked hard on the renovations—maybe too hard, because after a couple of years of shooting pains in her shoulder and multiple visits to the doctor, she was diagnosed with thoracic outlet syndrome. In June 2005, she had major neurosurgery and began a long path to rehabilitation.

Once she became ill, Mr. Danicic was anything but the supportive partner. In fact, he was very unhappy that she could not continue to work. She was, he said, "dragging him down." He refused to help her financially. She borrowed from her parents to meet her obligation to run the household, but by October of 2003, she had to move out because of his angry outbursts and verbal abuse.

By McLean's estimate, she had worked over 11,000 hours on the two properties and she asked in her court case for Mr. Danicic to give her a fair share of their value. His response?

- He accused her of blackmail.
- He told her he was seeing someone new.
- He denied that they were ever a couple and said that she had simply been a "tenant."
- He reported her to her insurers and accused her of filing fraudulent benefit claims.
- He caused the court case to require 18 separate court appearances.
- He claimed false debts to friends and ran up debt registered against the properties.
- He wrote threatening letters that were signed anonymously but for some reason included his own postal code.
- He threatened to release sexually explicit pictures to her family.

- He harassed her in numerous ways—even when he had "settled the case" he then refused to honour the settlement and caused more court appearances.
- He refused to co-operate with the court or to provide any evidence, even though during the course of the legal proceedings he had three different sets of lawyers.

In short, it was a legal and emotional nightmare.

Did they have a cohabitation agreement? No. Would things have been easier if they had one? Yes, I think so, because had such an agreement made it clear that Ms. McLean would not obtain an interest in the properties, she never would have started to work on them. On the other hand, if an agreement had stated that she was going to receive an interest in the properties, they could have quantified her entitlement in the cohabitation agreement. But because they never discussed these issues and were not aware of the legal rights and responsibilities that were involved, they ended up in a battle.

At the end of that battle, what did the judge do for Ms. McLean? The judge awarded her $106,000 for the work that she had done on the properties, including money for damages committed by Mr. Danicic. The judge also granted a restraining order against him and ordered that the two properties in his name be used as security to make sure that he paid the money owing to her. Over and above those amounts, the court ordered Mr. Danicic to pay in excess of $200,000 in legal fees. That's right, twice the amount that was recovered by Ms. McLean.

Now this was not your average case, to be sure, but it is an excellent illustration of the surprisingly bitter fighting that can result when a couple lives common law, blends their assets, works on and invests in each other's property, then splits without a plan. Ugly. Expensive. Avoidable.

WHY CANADIANS LIVE COMMON LAW

If you are, like hundreds of thousands of Canadians, living with someone or thinking about living with someone while you are not legally married, then this book is for you. To all outside appearances these "unmarried" relationships are no different than those of the people who went through the "formalities" of getting a marriage licence and having a full wedding to gain the status of "legal marriage." These unmarried couples may own their own homes, they may have children, they may be on the school committee and coach the children's sports teams, and they often look and act exactly like married couples. On the inside, their relationships are often no different than marriages—there is love, there is a commitment, and there are all the challenges of maintaining a solid relationship. The only thing missing is a marriage certificate.

Why would a Canadian couple choose to live together rather than get married? I mean, if the relationship looks just like a marriage and functions just like a marriage, why not actually get married? What is the difference? *The difference may be a very big one* and that's why I wrote this book. Canadians need to understand the legal consequences of living in a relationship and not being married.

But first, let's look at the six main reasons reasons people live together but don't get married.

1. I reject the idea of marriage on principle.

There are many people who see marriage as an unnecessary legal requirement, an expensive burden, an expensive commercial undertaking (i.e., the big wedding) rather than a loving exercise, and even, for some, a form of slavery. They feel that either you are committed or you are not; a marriage certificate won't make any difference. They choose not to be married, plain and simple. However, whether they made their decision to live together on principle or not, they still need this book.

2. I want to give the relationship a trial run before deciding on marriage.

This is a very common attitude, and quite logical. Why not give a relationship a test drive? Can you live together? Will you be able to make the compromises necessary? Young couples may be going straight from living in their parents' home to a live-in relationship. That can be tough if it's the first time they have actually had to work at a relationship. In some cases, the person may have lived on his or her own for a while and is unsure as to whether it is in them to make the necessary compromises that come along with sharing a home. Whether it is a trial run on the relationship or not, these people need this book.

3. I experienced a bad divorce in the past and just want to avoid the possibility of that happening again.

This is understandable. For couples like this, marriage equals inevitable pain. It was so tough to exit the first marriage, why would they attach that ball and chain again? In some cases, it may be that they watched their parents go through a painful divorce and consider marriage toxic. These couples choose to not marry out of fear, and whether they like it or not, they need this book.

4. I cannot get married because there is a legal impediment to doing so.

In order to get married, one must first apply for a marriage licence. In order to obtain the licence, a person must confirm that they are not already married. This means that if you were married but are not yet divorced, you cannot apply for a marriage licence. Many couples simply separate and never apply for their divorce. They move on into a cohabiting arrangement with a new partner. At some point they may wish to marry, but cannot do so until they complete the divorce from the previous partner. This may mean, for some people, that they have legal rights and responsibilities to a previous spouse to whom they are still legally married, *and* responsibilities to a common-law partner with whom they are currently cohabiting. These couples, perhaps more than anyone, need this book.

5. If I marry, I will lose a benefit that I need.

Some people are receiving a benefit by virtue of their legal status. In some cases, an individual who was previously married may be receiving spousal support (which used to be referred to as "alimony") and a remarriage will either trigger a termination of their entitlement to that spousal support, or at least a review of their entitlement. In other cases, a single parent may be receiving social benefits because of their marital status and cohabitation with a new partner may trigger either the loss of the benefit, or a review of their entitlement. For these people, remarriage or even cohabitation may be costly. In either case, they need this book.

6. Things are going fine—why would I rock the boat?

These couples are in perhaps the most dangerous position. They may have started their cohabitation as an experiment. In some cases they may not have even been in an intimate relationship but were rather simply roommates. The relationship then evolves into one of intimacy and continues. In some cases there may even be interruptions in the cohabitation. The couple may separate as one takes employment elsewhere, or moves, or travels extensively but then returns to the relationship. These couples are unconsciously creating what appears to be a committed relationship. The inertia carries them along, perhaps to a place of legal rights and responsibilities that they never intended or imagined. These people need this book.

If you fit into one or more of these categories, this book is for you.

TERMINOLOGY

Let's take a minute to look at some terminology. Most people have heard the expression "living common law" as a way of describing a couple—a man and a woman (more on the gender aspect later)—who are living together but not married. However, other terms have also been used (aside from the old term "living in sin"). Consider these terms: cohabitation, living together, common-law marriage, conjugal relationship (from the Latin *conjunctus*, to join), partners, living outside marriage, companionship, to name only a few. For the purposes of this book, I'm going to refer to these relationships as "living common law," as I believe this is the most common term. They are all variations on the same idea—living with a person but not married—but with a couple of important extra elements which we will look at in a moment.

The original of the expression "common-law marriage" can be traced back to English law where it was used to describe a situation in which a couple had not yet entered into their marriage but had entered into an agreement to marry at a later date. In other words, people agreed to live together before they got married. That term simply evolved into a description of people who decided to live together without any specific commitment to ultimately marry.

However, consider that we do not use any of the above terms to describe people in the following situations, which all involve unmarried people cohabitating::

- an older child who resides with and provides support to an elderly parent
- a person who resides as a caregiver with a person
- roommates at university or college
- two people sharing a two-bedroom apartment to save expenses
- a brother and a sister (or other siblings) sharing a home left to them by their parents

In Canada, we require an extra component to what we consider a common-law relationship: intimacy, and by that, I mean sexual intimacy and interdependence. Common-law relationships generally have the following elements:

1. A degree of length (which we will see varies from one part of Canada to the other)
2. Interdependence (again, the degree of dependence may vary)
3. An intimate nature, meaning there is an element of sexual intimacy (the frequency and details of the sexual component varies widely; in at least one case there was only one act of intercourse at the beginning of what became a lengthy relationship, but the court still considered it to be cohabitation that attracted legal rights and responsibilities)

These are the types of relationships with which we are concerned in this book, because these are the relationships that create legal rights and responsibilities for the couple. They need to know these rights and responsibilities, whether they are in such a relationship now or especially if they are thinking about entering one.

Why is it so important? Contrast a common-law couple's situation with a married couple. If a married couple splits or if someone dies, the laws of Canada provide a default system for helping them sort out legal issues around property and inheritance and so on. However, common-law couples do not have the same default system. They are forced into a position of proving and justifying their entitlement to anything that is not specifically registered in their name, and when it comes to estates it is even more complicated.

HOW MANY CANADIANS LIVE COMMON LAW?

While most committed relationships in Canada continue to be traditional marriages, the growth in the number of common-law relationships has been steadily accelerating. At the same time, growth in traditional marriages has been stagnating. In other words, common-law relationships are becoming more prevalent with each passing year. Let's take a look at the numbers provided by Statistics Canada which are based on information on Canadian families gathered between 2001 and 2006. In this five-year period, the number of "traditional" married couples grew by 6 percent, but the number of common-law couples grew by 19 percent—more than three times the rate. By the year 2020, half of all couples will be common law. In other words, half will be married and half will be living common law. The people who are choosing common-law cohabitation are not just younger Canadians; older people in their sixties and beyond are choosing not to marry and to live together instead. Their attitude seems to be one of "Marriage? Been there, done that." They are not fussy about the need for a formal legal commitment.

The numbers provided by Statistics Canada also show some interesting trends in *where* in Canada common-law unions are becoming the most prevalent. Quebec, for example, represents 44 percent of Canada's total number of common-law unions as of 2006, versus 10 percent in Ontario and Prince Edward Island, respectively. The Yukon, the Northwest Territories, and Nunavut also have much higher numbers of couples living common law, with the percentage being about 25 percent.

The bottom line: more and more Canadians are living common law. They all have their reasons for doing so. They need to know what they are getting into, because legal rights and responsibilities are being created everyday.

And while we think about the legal rights and responsibilities we are getting into, let's do some due diligence on the person with whom you are about to live, or the person with whom you already live as a partner.

2

EYES WIDE OPEN: DUE DILIGENCE AND RELATIONSHIP BUILDING

~

Before we examine the "legal parts" of common-law living, let's look at the "people parts." You are making an important decision when you commit to cohabiting with someone. Do you really know the person with whom you are about to share your life?

WHY DUE DILIGENCE?

If you were starting a new business with a partner or buying a business from someone, you would do what business people refer to as "due diligence." You would check out the potential partner. You would investigate thoroughly the books of the business that you are going to buy. You would make sure your money and your future are safe. The same approach should apply to relationships: make sure your future is safe. What should you be looking for? There are three areas of potential concern: health, criminal activity and financial problems. Let's take a look at each of them.

Your Partner's Health

When we think of a person's health we tend to think of physical injuries, illness or diseases. Those kinds of challenges are common for all of us. However, mental health issues can be just as daunting for couples and families. In this section I want to look at some of the key considerations as you do due diligence with respect to both types of health. Let's start with "physical."

Physical Health

Poor health can be hard on a relationship. Ask yourself honestly if you are prepared to stay in a relationship with someone who would require your care and support for a serious health challenge. Are you prepared to be in a relationship when you perhaps will carry the entire financial burden because your partner is too ill to work? I know this sounds harsh, but I have seen these types of challenges undermine a relationship very quickly. Disease, injury, illness—are any of these a factor in your partner's life? Any evidence that they may play a role in his or her family's life? Are there illnesses that your children might inherit given your partner's family history? Have you been open with your partner about disclosing your potential health challenges? What if your partner reveals to you that she or he has AIDS, multiple sclerosis, lupus, cancer, or any one of a number of devastating diseases? What would your decision about living together be if you learned that your partner's family has been devastated by breast cancer, or that your partner's family has a long history of alcoholism?

I'm not suggesting that this information should automatically result in an end to the relationship, but knowing about it before you commit to the relationship allows you to go into it with your eyes wide open. If and when these health challenges emerge, at least you knew what you might be in for in the relationship. Bottom line: learn about your partner's health and your partner's family's health, and answer honestly and completely the questions that are asked of you about your health and that of your family. Put it all on the table so that you both go into the relationship with your eyes wide open.

Mental Health

This type of health challenge is even more difficult. Here is an example of a real-life shocker that I encountered: a young couple began living together and everything was great for the first few years. Suddenly, she began to behave a little out of character. She went on wild shopping sprees to the United States and had casual sexual relations with strangers. She developed financial problems. She became depressed. She went through mood swings, and suddenly there were violent episodes. Her partner was in shock—what was happening to their relationship? The answer: she had stopped taking her antidepressant medication. He had no idea that she had been taking medication because she had kept her illness a secret. Was that fair to him? I don't think so. As a result, he was unwilling to work with her to restore some stability to her life and the relationship ended.

In the relationships that lawyers see going sour, mental health issues often loom large. I was involved in a case in which one partner suffered from obsessive compulsive disorder (OCD), which meant that, for her, non-stop cleaning of their home was absolutely necessary. The extent of her problem was not obvious until they were living together for several months, but gradually it became worse and worse. He noticed when he came home from work that their home now reeked of bleach. Suddenly, newspapers were forbidden in the house because they contained "germs." Similarly, no shoes were allowed in the house, and then *no people* were allowed in the house. Furniture was covered and they ate in the basement. Her OCD was out of control.

Would you want to know your partner suffered from that disorder before you started living together? Probably. What if your partner has schizophrenia, or suffers from manic depression? Wouldn't you want to know about it before you moved in? Me too. Bottom line: learn about your partner's mental health and their family's mental health background. Is there a history of depression in the family? Have there been suicides? These are valuable pieces of information that can help you understand what kind of relationship you may end up having with your partner. Both of you should put it all on the table and go into the relationship with your eyes wide open about any potential mental health challenges that may be down the road.

Criminal Problems

Knowing about your partner's past criminal activities or convictions is absolutely critical. In one situation that I encountered, a couple who had been living together for several years and had two children set off on the children's dream trip to Florida and Disney World. For months the husband had resisted the trip. He had many excuses—too much work, not feeling well enough to make the trip. But he finally gave in after the children and their mother insisted that this particular March break, they were going to Disney World—no excuses. At the border they were stopped and, after having their passports and ID checked, were told to turn their car around and head back home. They were not granted access to the United States. Why? The husband had multiple convictions for fraud and a narcotics conviction to boot. He had simply been avoiding the border because he knew that his convictions could block access to the United States. The wife had no idea. It was his little secret about his past, a secret of which he was ashamed and had kept from her. She also now understood why he had turned down that great job offer that would have meant travel to the United States from time to time. How do you think she felt? What else had he kept secret? The relationship suffered.

What kinds of criminal activity have been discovered by couples after they began cohabiting? Consider the following situations other couples faced:

- His love of bicycling was not really related to his desire to help the environment but was simply because he had lost his licence after a conviction for impaired driving. His employment prospects were very limited geographically.
- She had been fired from a company and convicted of fraud for falsifying invoices and defrauding the business of thousands of dollars. She could never get hired for anything but casual jobs.
- He had several criminal charges and one conviction for assault against a previous wife. He could not travel to the United States.
- She had an accident in which someone was seriously injured while she drove without insurance. Her licence had been suspended for impaired driving. Now she was unable to get car insurance and the lawsuit had bankrupted her.

- He stole a friend's credit card and was convicted of fraud.
- She wrote bad cheques to a landlord.
- He had a gambling problem and a conviction for carrying a concealed weapon.
- She had a conviction for criminal harassment because she had stalked an old boyfriend and damaged his car by flattening all the tires.

Shall I go on? Wouldn't you rather know about these things before you start making commitments to each other? Bottom line: have a frank discussion with your partner and learn about their past and specifically about any problems they have had with the law.

Financial Problems

This is a big one. What do you really know about your partner's financial past, his or her earning capabilities, and ability to manage money? Over the years I have encountered couples who work as a team on their financial situation. They share information, invest together and prosper together. However, I have also seen some spectacular financial screw-ups that have devastated couples. Why? Because one of them operated in a "secret financial world." Consider the following true stories. How would you feel in these situations?

- A couple's jointly-held home is now in jeopardy because she hadn't paid her income taxes for several years.
- A couple needs to pay off a mortgage and a line of credit, which will take years, because he decided he knew enough about investing in the stock market simply from reading the newspaper and watching TV, then lost a bundle.
- He had been fired from multiple jobs because "he can't work with others" and now had trouble finding a job.
- It turned out she was not a "brilliant entrepreneur" who has simply had bad luck, but a serial business flop who is now about to go bankrupt for the second time.
- He bought an expensive time-share in South America on their joint credit card, but now they cannot afford the airfare needed to get to this country, so the investment was a waste of money.

- She doesn't have a credit card, not because she is against them (as she always says), but because her credit rating has been ruined and no institution will give her one.
- They can't buy a home because they don't qualify for a mortgage. He has a huge debt for unpaid taxes.

Many Canadians simply do not know how to manage money. Would you want to know that before or after you start living together? I thought so. Bottom line: learn about your partner's financial situation, their job history, bankruptcies, credit card history; do the equivalent of a credit check on them. One analyst refers to these kinds of financial problems as "FTDs." Instead of having sexually transmitted diseases, a couple experiences "financially transmitted diseases." Go into your relationship with eyes wide open; there should be no financial surprises.

~

Now, I realize that dealing with these issues may not be what many would view as an "enjoyable" or "easy" conversation to have with their partner. No one likes the idea of confronting their partner about the unpleasant details of their past, the personal and potentially upsetting health history of their family, or sensitive issues such as money management. But *do not* let it deter you from making a commitment to learn such details about your partner. I've seen too many relationships ruined because partners didn't make the effort to find out important details about each other's health, family history, and financial situation. When the gory details ultimately did emerge, they wished they had known sooner. You owe it to yourself and to your partner to make sure that you are both aware of any potentially serious issues that may arise. And this doesn't necessarily mean interrogating each other about the details. As a starting point, a little online research could be valuable—Google your future partner!

Certainly, you will learn some details by addressing them in an open conversation with your partner, but other details will come to light simply by being attentive. When you're at family functions, make an effort to talk to your partner's relatives and listen to stories they tell, and pay attention to the subjects that are no-no's. You may find out about a long-running family illness, or they may hint at a past problem that you can discuss later with your partner (for example, if relatives keep telling you that "You're the best thing that ever happened to him/her," find out why). Above all, what's important is that you are in a relationship in which you both appreciate the value of full disclosure and can have an open and honest conversation about such tough issues as a result of that disclosure. Ignore these important personal details at your peril!

So, let's assume that you have done your due diligence. You are now fully aware of all important issues and challenges in the relationship, and let's assume that you are now still committed to this relationship. What next? Are you ready to work at the relationship every day? In the next section, I provide some observations about ways to develop and maintain a good relationship.

RELATIONSHIP BUILDING

I have seen my fair share of divorces and breakdowns in common-law relationships over the last three decades during which I've practised law. I have witnessed some very ugly separations and represented people in court battles over children, property, and money. I have seen couples spend hundreds of thousands of dollars on lawyers. I have seen weddings called off, children put in foster care, and their parents sent to jail. In some cases, I have helped grandparents fight their own children in order to get custody of their grandchildren, and I have seen it all up-close including blood, bruises, bankruptcy, and tears. And after it is all over, I have seen those same people pick themselves up, dust themselves off, and start over in a new relationship. Maybe I have only seen the relationships that have gone bad or people behaving at their absolute worst, but after witnessing the collapse of so many relationships, I have a better understanding of what can make or break a relationship.

One lesson that I have drawn from these observations is that couples rarely work at their relationships as hard as they do at their jobs, at their businesses, at their careers, and in some cases, even at their hobbies. They leave the success or failure of their relationships to chance. In this section I want to provide a little guidance on what I think it takes to have a good relationship that is not only loving, but also durable. Let's start by taking a look at the 10 elements that make up the foundation of a good relationship: (1) honesty, (2) patience, (3) taking the long view, (4) respect, (5) balance, (6) tolerance and forgiveness, (7) room for growth, (8) a sense of humour, (9) loving gestures, (10) effort. In my view, if any one of these key elements is missing then the love upon which this relationship is based is not mature and the relationship is therefore at risk. Are you or your partner dishonest, impatient, short-sighted, or disrespectful? Is one in the couple more powerful than the other? Are you forgiving? Is the relationship stagnant? Are you unable to laugh at yourselves? Is the relationship cold? Are you not prepared to work at it? If the answer is yes to any one of these, it can be fatal to the relationship.

What Makes for a Mature Relationship?

As a divorce lawyer for the last 30 years I have seen relationships both good and bad. I have seen the problems that eat away at a relationship, that undermine and corrode what might otherwise be a successful couple. In my view it depends in large part on whether the underlying love between the people is mature. In this section I invite you to consider some key components to a mature relationship.

1. Honesty

In my experience, dishonesty is the #1 cause of problems in relationships, and in many cases it begins long before the couple has made a decision to live together. I spoke earlier in this chapter about the need for due diligence. Hiding health problems, a criminal past, or financial problems as one goes into a relationship is dishonesty. Similarly, if those problems develop only after the relationship has begun but they are hidden from a spouse, then there is dishonesty within the relationship and it is at risk.

2. Patience

Patience means different things to different people. For some, it is as simple as waiting a few extra minutes for someone to come around to sharing their view. For others, patience can mean waiting an entire year for a situation within the relationship to evolve. In a good relationship, it means being patient for small things and for big things, and can mean giving your partner as much time as it takes him or her to do whatever it is that's important to them.

In one case that I saw, a man had to be very patient while his intelligent, beautiful, and well-educated partner decided what was important to her. Her life seemed to have been pre-determined for her; she was successful and happy. However, when she reached her fortieth birthday, she was suddenly unsure about what to do with her future. The things that she had worked on before did not seem important anymore and she needed time to decide what she would do next. After a couple of months, he became a little restless about her uncertainty. She had quit her job and they were missing her income. He was worried that she was slipping into a depression, but he waited and supported her as she worked out her priorities. And then suddenly, she had worked it out; it was time to become a teacher. She enrolled in teachers' college, attained her degree, and went on to become a happy teacher—and a happy partner. His patience was a virtue in that circumstance.

3. *Taking the Long View*

Therapists who assist couples spend a great deal of time trying to identify the indicators of a good relationship. They want to be able to tell people in therapy that this type of behaviour or that type of behaviour is good or bad. One of the good behaviours that they have identified is the ability to take the long view of the relationship. Where the individuals involved see their commitment as long term, they are better able to endure the little bumps that challenge them along the way. In fact, many successful couples acknowledge that the longer the relationship lasts and the more challenges they face successfully, the easier it is to roll over fresh obstacles.

Once I met a couple who described suffering a real blow early in their relationship. Just as they were preparing to embark on what they thought would be a happy, prosperous life together, the financial bottom fell out of the husband's successful business. It went bankrupt very suddenly, through no fault of his own. However, the couple worked through it, and all the stress that goes with financial problems. They rebuilt the business as partners and, as a result, the relationship became, in their mind, indestructible. They both felt that having been through the experience together, and taking the long view, they could now withstand any challenge.

4. Respect

Respect is so much bigger in a relationship than any dictionary definition could capture. What makes us hold our partner in a place of honour? Perhaps we see in them qualities that we admire, qualities that we wish we had. Respecting your partner may be something as basic as simply wanting to know what they think before you make a decision because you value the extra insight that they bring to a problem. Unfortunately, many couples appreciate the importance of respect only after it has disappeared.

I will never forget meeting a man who conveyed to me in an ashamed whisper that he and his partner were trying to work things out after his affair with a co-worker became public in a most humiliating way. The co-worker had launched into a drunken tirade against his partner at an office function. After the ugly incident, he was very remorseful and determined to set the matter right, but he knew that something was different with his partner. He sounded wounded as he described it to me: "She has no respect for me any more." A state of being held in honour was gone.

5. Balance

The old expression about everything in moderation certainly holds true for relationships. Whether it is the level of power between the two partners, their career objectives, or other activities, balance is always needed. I have seen couples separate because a husband's career became a single-minded obsession for him, or because a wife's devotion to a new religious faith became her sole purpose in life, and in one case, because a person's devotion to a new hobby—cycling—became the focal point of all their spare time. A balanced lifestyle is a solid foundation to a lasting relationship. Similarly, if one spouse begins to dominate the relationship or, on the other hand, one is not making an equal contribution, then other elements of the relationship may suffer as well. Will respect for a partner continue for very long if one dominates the other? Will there be room for growth? Why would spouses take the long view in a relationship if the relationship is not really about their life at all? Can people be honest in a relationship in which they have no power? Not for long.

6. *Tolerance and Forgiveness*

This aspect of relationship-building needs little explanation, but couples should understand that it is called for in the most subtle situations. The beauty of a relationship is the security and safety that I mentioned earlier. That security includes the freedom to make some mistakes as the relationship grows and as we grow as people, and know that one partner is still in your corner rooting for you, tolerating your shortcomings and sometimes, forgiving the booboos you make along the way.

7. *Room for Growth*

I don't think that a person's core values change very much over the course of their life, but there are changes in us nonetheless. All of the challenges and experiences that one encounters over the course of a lifetime contribute to a person's growth as an individual. The hard part can be giving a partner the room to grow when it sometimes pushes you out of a comfortable routine. Imagine, for example, a powerful businessperson who had been in a relationship of 15 years suddenly developing a passionate interest in homelessness. An incident in his life had stirred up something dormant. He went from spending his evenings in a tux at business meetings and cocktail receptions to wearing a comfortable pair of corduroy pants and sweaters and working in shelters for the homeless. Gradually, he began to apply all of his know-how and business savvy to the non-profit voluntary sector. His earnings took a hit but he had never been happier. His wife noticed a profound change, not only in his level of activity, but also in his level of happiness. He had not changed, but he had grown.

Life can settle into some comfortable grooves and we don't like to fiddle with a good thing. It is understandable that if one partner starts to rock the boat a little bit, then the other one may resist it. But if you are patient and flexible and allow that room to grow, it will pay dividends and you will both grow together.

8. *A Sense of Humour*

It helps to have a lot of laughter in one's life and it certainly helps relationships. The need for a sense of humour is most often called for in relation to one's self. In other words, we all need to be reminded not to take ourselves too seriously. A sense of humour can come to the rescue in the most difficult times.

9. *Loving Gestures*

In 1994, the results of a very interesting study of couples in marriage therapy were published. This study (called the Gottman study) was drawn from work done over a 20-year period with two thousand couples and even involved the observation and measurement of their responses to each other while in therapy. Videotapes were examined to monitor facial expressions and language. The study was quite comprehensive and the results blew away many of the assumptions that marriage therapists and others have about which relationships will work and which ones won't. Gottman is so confident in his research that he claims he can predict with a 94-percent accuracy rate which relationships will end and which will not.

Gottman points out that we all tend to look at relationships in which there is a lot of arguing and shouting and assume "Well, that will never last—they argue too much." Likewise, it is not uncommon to hear friends and family say, "They're not compatible … it's a different religion, a different ethnic background, a different class, different tastes. It can't last." These are not necessarily the indicators of a so-called good relationship. There is something else at work in the relationships; something inside the intimacy of the relationship itself.

One of the key findings of the Gottman study is the "Five-to-One Rule." Relationships are based on interactions between the couple, good and bad. Gottman found that he could quantify the ratio of positive to negative interactions needed to keep a relationship in good shape. He found that satisfied couples, no matter how their relationship stacked up against the ideal, were those who maintained a five-to-one ratio of positive to negative moments.

In the course of a day, there are opportunities for good and bad moments with your partner. Do you choose to tell your partner that they are attractive, or do you make a sarcastic remark about how they're not keeping in shape the way they used to? Do you encourage your partner to set aside time for themselves and their personal interests, or do you only remind them of their obligations and duties in the relationship? Do you make time for personal time away from the kids, or do you take turns handing off the responsibility until you each feel like rotating daycare shift workers. Do you smile at each other? Do you even look at each other? These are all the little positive and negative interactions of the day. Can you keep them in a ratio of five positives for every one negative? Can you afford not to? You can have a bad moment in a relationship but you need to balance it with five good ones. It is a lot like keeping a healthy balance in the bank—some protection for a rainy day in the relationship.

10. Effort

Success in relationships, as in everything else, takes work. Couples cannot take their relationships for granted. The world throws a lot more at a couple these days than it did in the past. Be prepared to put in the effort, to be on guard, and to be ready to tackle the problems that will inevitably come.

Have Realistic Expectations

Let's take a look now at another aspect of having a good relationship—realistic expectations. During the course of any relationship, many things can and will happen. The following is a short list of things that I have actually seen happen to couples and that could just as easily happen to you:

- a serious illness—mental or physical
- injury in a car accident
- deafness or blindness

- termination of employment
- criminal activity and a resulting prison sentence
- addiction to drugs or alcohol
- money lost due to gambling
- a big lottery win
- transfer of employment to another country
- deportation
- an affair
- sexual abuse of a child
- an extended disappearance
- accidental death of a child due to drinking and driving

All of these things have happened to someone just like you. People in love say that they will be able to handle anything that comes their way. Could you handle some of the things on the above list? Some relationships rise to the challenge, many do not. The bottom line is this: having realistic expectations in a relationship does not mean that you are cynical or jaded about people and life. It means that you are simply aware that anything can happen—anything.

Having said that, let's look in particular at some of the more common challenges.

Money

Financial problems are quite common and often lead to stress in a relationship. Canadians have suffered from a record number of bankruptcies, job losses, and debt levels and the recent economic troubles have really taken a toll on Canadian families. No one likes to tell their partner or their children that they can't have a computer, that their vacation is cancelled, that the car cannot be repaired, or that the house has to be sold. Poor finances make people feel trapped and helpless.

On the other side of the coin, we have couples who have problems because they have too much money—that's right, too much. I saw a couple with children blow apart because they could not handle a lot of money that came into their hands very suddenly. Before long, the money was gone—and so was the relationship. Couples need to have realistic expectations and all couples, especially younger ones, should get some basic financial planning advice. Speak to your bank representative, follow the advice of trusted friends, and shop around for someone who is qualified, experienced and honest to advise you on financial matters. There are many very good financial planners out there (check out, for example, www.fpsc.ca). Something as simple as a good working financial budget can make a big difference in eliminating stress in a relationship.

What follows is a list of 10 tips that are designed to help make it easier to find a financial planner, courtesy of the Financial Planning Standards Council (www.fpsccanada.org):

- Know what you want. Determine your general financial goals and specific needs, such as insurance, estate planning, and investment planning.
- Be prepared. Do a little research on financial planning strategies and terminology.
- Get advisor referrals from colleagues and friends.
- Look for competence. There are many degrees and designations. The Financial Planning Standards Council recommends a planner with a CFP designation (Certified Financial Planner).
- Interview more than one planner. Ask about their education, experience and specialties, the size and duration of their practice, client communications, and whether assistants handle client matter.
- Check their background. Call their professional associations to check on their complaint record.
- Ask for references from other professionals, such as accountants, insurance agents, or legal advisors who work with the planner.
- Ask for a registration or disclosure document detailing method of compensation, conflicts of interest, business affiliations, and personal qualifications.
- Request a written advisory contract or engagement letter.
- Reassess the relationship regularly.

Children

Ideally, a couple should decide before they commit to their relationship about the question of raising a family together. The realistic expectation here is simply this: if you cannot agree in advance about whether you both want to have children, under no circumstances should you get married, and it should put a real question mark over whether you want to live in a common-law relationship until the issue is sorted out—honestly.

Relatives

You will recall from the above list of characteristics that contribute to a good relationship the need for patience and tolerance. This may have no greater application than when one is dealing with in-laws. The need to have some realistic expectations can arise in a couple of different situations. You may have heard the expression "the sandwich generation" —these are Canadians in their thirties, forties, and fifties who are sandwiched in between caring for their own children and their aging parents, and in some cases, grandparents. This group will grow larger and larger over the next few decades, and it will mean an extra strain on many relationships. Imagine trying to squeeze into an already crowded schedule the need to pop into a nursing home to care for your mother or father. In many cases, they may be living right in your home with an additional expense for nursing care. Now, imagine that it is not you but your spouse who must add the extra care onto the daily routine. Remember the comfortable routine and the room for growth we talked about earlier? Both can evaporate in this kind of heat.

Studies of this growing social issue have shown that parental care generally falls to the women in the family. We already know that women are still doing the majority of the housework and childcare, and when eldercare is added to the situation it will feel less like a sandwich and more like a vise. Take a look at your own situation and that of your spouse. How would you handle that kind of responsibility? Talk about it.

A second in-law issue is the one on which many comedians have made a living: the dreaded in-laws who meddle and try to run their children's lives after they start their relationships. Unfortunately, the jokes have a basis in reality, and I have seen some terrible interference in relationships by parents. Rarely do all four parents get into it; more often than not, the strong personalities in the parents' marriages are the ones who try to become overly involved in their children's relationships.

As you head into a relationship you have to have realistic expectations about family members who will intervene in your life together. Ideally, you have had a chance to meet the families involved and size them up. A relative who meddles and tries to control their child before the relationship even begins will not suddenly stop doing so after you are living together. For example, if a young man has lived in his parents' basement for ten years, saving his money up for a nice car while his mother does the cooking and cleaning for him, don't expect things to be much different once a common-law relationship begins. Have realistic expectations about your relationship—not just with your partner, but with your partner's family.

Careers

The need for realistic expectations in our careers doesn't need much explanation to most Canadians. We have all been through the recent economic difficulties and understand the way in which global markets can turn our economy upside-down overnight. We hear constant warnings about flu pandemics, terrorism, and other threats around the globe. The situation can be rosy one day and suddenly go quite sour. We need to have realistic expectations about the security of our own financial position.

A neighbour of mine sold his house on the condition that the purchasers could arrange financing within 72 hours. That is a pretty common condition in a house transaction; however, when the intended purchaser went to her employer to get a letter for the bank confirming her earnings, she got a pink slip instead. She lost her dream home and her job in the same day. Be realistic about what can happen to your career and how it can affect your plans.

Illness

I mentioned this aspect of relationships earlier in the context of due diligence. It can be a shocker when a relationship has to face illness or injury (and let's not forget that it's a dangerous world out there—car accidents, workplace accidents, crime, and other dangers are all around us). It would be a miracle if we got through life without something happening. When we consider the thousands of illnesses from which Canadians suffer, physically and mentally, it can be a little overwhelming.

Having realistic expectations in a relationship means understanding that these things could happen to you or your spouse. Could you cope? Could your partner? There are couples who simply cannot deal with these kinds of challenges. I once met with a client whose wife had left him the day after he was diagnosed with cancer. For whatever reason, she could not handle the prospect of seeing him through that ordeal. And that case is not an isolated one. Lawyers see many cases in which illness or injury end a relationship. It is sad, but true. The bottom line is be realistic about what life can and will throw at you as an individual and as a couple.

Develop Good Problem-Solving Skills

Good problem-solving skills are about having the ability to handle reality when it hits day after day. Marriage therapists and lawyers will tell you that the best indicator of whether a relationship will be successful is not the challenges of money, sex, or any of the usual problems we often associate with relationships. It is the willingness and ability of both partners to work on problems and to solve them. Then it won't matter what is thrown your way, because if you work on solving the problem together, your relationship has a good chance of being successful. Don't wish that you won't have problems, because that is unrealistic. Wish instead that you will have the ability to work on them together when they arrive—and trust me, they will.

Ten Elements of Good Problem Solving

There is an approach to problem solving that can be of great assistance to a couple in their relationship. It is simple and it consists of identifying the real problem and its origins, proposing alternative solutions, evaluating those alternatives, picking the one that meets both spouses' needs, and then implementing it. Let's look at it in more detail through the following ten elements:

1. *What is the problem?*

As a couple, you should be prepared to ask really simple questions about the challenges or problems that you think you face. Do you both come up with the same answer? Let me give you an example. If a couple is facing serious financial problems and they ask themselves what the problem really is, they may not get the same answer. The husband might say that the problem is "We don't earn enough money and I need a better paying job." The wife, on the other hand, might say, "We spend too much on things that we don't need, things that are not important or that we cannot afford. Let's keep our jobs and spend less." They don't see the same problem and they cannot begin to solve it until they agree on what the problem truly is.

2. *How did this problem arise?*

What is its source? It can be very helpful to trace the origin of a problem. Has this come up before? Why is it happening again? Are we repeating mistakes that have been made before? For example, if overspending led to an enormous debt, and the debt was then consolidated into a new mortgage on the home in the past, but now another period of overspending has allowed another debt to balloon, did the consolidation really solve the underlying problem? If the couple can pin down the source of the problem, they may prevent the problem from happening again.

3. *What are the facts of which we are absolutely certain?*

A couple cannot possibly hope to solve a problem if they do not have all of the facts surrounding the issue. This means that, in analyzing the problem, the couple must ask, "Do we have enough information?" Remember the advice about honesty in the relationship. It applies here as well. All of the facts need to be on the table for a proper solution to be developed.

4. Once all of the facts have been gathered, does the problem look the same?

Don't be surprised if it looks a lot different after a true picture has been assembled. This means that once you have all of the facts in hand, go back to the question that we started with: "What is the problem?"

5. What are the timelines we face in solving this problem?

Are they rigid or flexible? The way that you choose to solve the problem and the alternatives that you may consider will be influenced by the time limits imposed by others. If a creditor is forcing your hand, then making a career change to earn more money may not be realistic. If one of you has been offered a job in another country and must give an answer by a certain date, then your choices are limited. Be aware of time restrictions on your decision making.

6. What are the alternative ways in which we can solve this problem?

Never assume that there is only one solution because, more often than not, there are several ways to solve the problem. A couple of the solutions may not seem suitable, but they are at least possibilities. Be open-minded, brainstorm about possibilities, think out loud, and imagine the best solution if it were entirely up to you. Don't be afraid to involve other professionals, such as financial planners, lawyers, or your accountant in developing a solution.

7. What are the pros and cons of each alternative?

This can be quite a useful exercise as you both work at listing the advantages and disadvantages of each potential solution. Sometimes, you will be surprised at how easily the best alternative emerges.

8. Which alternative makes the most sense?

Depending on the kind of problem you face, the option that looks the best to you might not be the same for your partner. It will be necessary to consider what is best for the relationship, rather than what is best for you as individuals.

9. *What does my partner think?*

Hopefully you will both have the same information in front of you, have identified the same problem, have considered the same options, and considered the same pros and cons for each option. This is the time to make sure that each partner is given an opportunity to say what he or she thinks about a possible solution. Don't jump to conclusions and start figuring out how to implement the solution unless you are certain that both of you are committed to implementing it.

10. *Are we committed to implementing the solution?*

Assuming that you are both on the same wavelength about the best alternative to solve the problem, you must both commit yourselves to working on implementation. Finding the correct approach is only half the answer. It must still be implemented and it must be implemented together. Leaving the problem solving to just one partner will create an imbalance in the relationship and may very well lead to a repetition of the mistake that got you into the problem in the first place.

~

In this chapter we looked at why a lot of relationships go sour. Good relationships are built from the bottom up based on mature love, realistic expectations, and good problem-solving skills. Couples can learn to have realistic expectations and they can learn to be good problem solvers, but when it comes to having the mature love required as a foundation, there are some limitations on how much can be learned. A person is either committed to those elements of a mature love—or not. I hope that some of the questions posed in this chapter will help you as a couple in evaluating each other and in evaluating the challenges that you face over the years together.

3

RIGHTS AND RESPONSIBILITIES TO EACH OTHER WHILE LIVING TOGETHER

Let's consider what you are getting into simply by making the decision to move in together. Whether you live together for a year or for 25, whether you later separate or not, you are assuming rights and responsibilities simply by entering an unmarried relationship.

WHEN DOES COHABITATION BEGIN?

One of the biggest differences between marriage and living common law is the ability to determine the launch date. Married couples have an actual certificate or marriage licence and there is rarely any doubt about when their life together began. Common-law couples often begin their lives in a vague or gradual way. Consider the following situations:

- Bob and Allison had been dating for a year off and on and shared a house while at university in Victoria with three other students. However, the other roommates moved out and Bob and Allison stayed in the house for two years, eventually sharing the same room and bed as a couple.

- Karen and James each have their own apartments in Toronto, but they spend five to six nights a week at Karen's place because James's roommates are too rowdy. They have been doing this for a couple of years.
- Alexa and Curtis live in a condo in Calgary, but rarely see each other because they are pilots for different airlines. They plan to marry, though, as soon as their schedules coincide. They're lucky if they overlap two or three nights a month at their condo.
- Janice has been out of work and is couch surfing in Halifax. She has been surfing at Sylvia's place now for six months and things are getting romantic, at least that's what Sylvia hopes.
- Ricco and Kate have been dating for a year. It has gone from sleepovers to moving in over the last three months.

I could go on with dozens of examples. Do the above cohabitations look like common-law relationships? Should legal rights and responsibilities be created by these living arrangements? Does each person have to be on the same page as to what is happening?

I received a call at the office one day from a Toronto woman who was "double checking" some information about common-law couples. Among other queries, she asked how long a person needed to live with someone in order to claim half of the person's assets. I was a little shocked at how mercenary she was in her questioning. I explained that, in Ontario, common-law couples have no statutory rights to claim a half interest in a partner's property. She insisted that once you were "common law" property was 50/50, "just like married people" after one year. Wrong, I explained.

I asked her how long she had been living with this person. Her answer: 13 months, 22 days. Her sole motive was to gain access to assets.

Were these two people on the same page about their rights and responsibilities? I doubt it.

Canadian courts have had to sort these issues out because, as we will see in upcoming sections, without a cohabitation agreement, common-law couples need to trace and retrace their steps to determine "who bought what when" and to be able to answer the question "When did our cohabitation really begin?"

As the courts try to sort these issues out, they look at questions such as these:

- Are their names on a lease, rent cheque or other documents that would evidence the beginning of cohabitation?
- When did one person give up their accommodation to live in the other's accommodation?
- Did a person maintain a separate address?
- Did they bank or invest together?
- When were they both sharing shelter?
- Was there intimacy? When did sexual relations start?
- Was there an engagement? Marriage planning?
- Did they socialize as a couple?
- Was there a division of labour in the household?
- Did they have meals together? What would their neighbours and family say if asked?
- Were they at family Christmas celebrations or holidays together? Did they vacation together?
- Did one person pay all the expenses for the couple?
- Was this just a casual or experimental relationship?
- What were their intentions?

As the court sifts through the answer to these and other questions, a common denominator usually emerges—a date when they were living together in a committed relationship.

Ideally, for the court to make a finding of a spousal relationship, that finding requires consensual acceptance by two people of each other as spouses and that such acceptance was declared by each person to each other in both words and actions.

It is possible that a court might treat a couple as being common law for legal purposes, even though one of them declares that he or she had absolutely no intention of being in a common-law relationship. In other words, one person says it is serious and going some place and the other swears it was just causal and experimental. One person's declaration of a lack of intention will not prevent a legal finding of a common-law status. Are you starting to see why cohabitation agreements can be useful?

Let's turn now to a consideration of what types of rights and responsibilities a couple takes on once this relationship begins. At this stage, let's leave out considerations about what happens in the event of death or if the couple splits. For now, we will simply take a look at what happens once you begin to cohabit, because it is during that phase of cohabitation that dependency begins to appear. In this next section, we will consider what happens with respect to children, property, employment, benefits, income tax, and even wills and powers of attorney.

WHAT ABOUT HAVING CHILDREN?

No one needs a marriage licence to have children, and certainly common-law couples in Canada are having children, as well as blending children that they have had in a previous relationships into a new relationship. There is little difference in the parenting obligations of common-law and married couples as it relates to their own biological children, but step-parenting can be complicated. First and foremost, there will probably be another biological parent involved in the lives of the children. Perhaps that parent has joint custody or access to the children on a regular basis and the time the children spend with the new common-law family can be interrupted regularly. If there are two sets of children being blended, then co-ordination of three or more households may be required. Discipline can also be an issue, especially when there are two different styles of parenting and children see an inconsistent approach. One parent is sometimes viewed as being "too harsh" or "spoiling the children." It is a very delicate issue and it calls for patience and diplomacy—with the children, with the common-law partner, and the other biological parent.

Provincial family law also addresses a situation that we sometimes see in the classified section of a newspaper. Have you ever wondered about those little ads that say "Bill Brown will not be responsible for the debts of Betty Brown"? These ads are supposed to be evidence to the world that a husband will not pay bills incurred by his spouse. Its origins are in Section 45 of Ontario's *Family Law Act* which states the following:

> During cohabitation a spouse [and this includes common-law spouses] has authority to render himself or herself and his or her spouse jointly and severally liable to a third party for necessities of life *unless* the spouse has notified the third party that he or she has withdrawn the authority.

This means a common-law spouse has a financial obligation to provide the necessities of life while cohabiting, meaning food, shelter, medical needs, and clothing. He or she will have to pay bills incurred for such items unless the authority is withdrawn by the spouse who is expected to pay the bills. The same obligation exists with respect to a child. If the child incurs expenses for food, shelter, medical needs or clothing, the parents must pay those bills. However, in the case of children, that authority cannot be taken away.

If you live common law and blend children into the family, this question arises: What is the non-biological parent's obligation for his or her common-law partner's children while the family is intact? Married couples often adopt their partner's children from a previous relationship. However, in my experience, it has been unusual to see common-law partners adopt the children of their spouse. Common-law step-parents, who have not adopted their partner's children, technically have no rights with respect to those children, but they may have responsibilities. For the most part, the step-parent cannot be forced to pay for the child's schooling or medical needs, they cannot go to the children's school and remove the child from school property, and they cannot remove the child from Canada without the permission of the child's biological parent. If the common-law partner has sole custody of their children, then that parent can delegate responsibility to a common-law step-parent (e.g., provide a letter authorizing the parent to remove a child from school property or even from the country). But this is an authority given by the parent. There are no direct rights vis-à-vis the child.

This can sometimes be an issue in terms of discipline. Does a common-law step-parent have any more authority over their partner's children other than that to which the biological parent agrees or to which the child consents? Morally, perhaps, but legally, no. The relationship between common-law step-parents and step-children can be tricky. But as we will see, it is also something that can benefit from clarification in a cohabitation agreement.

Financially, caring for children varies from family to family and depends largely on the parents' respective abilities to contribute. If incomes are equal, life may be a little less complicated. If the common-law couple is caring for their own biological children, their finances with respect to those children will be no different than any other family. However, when the common-law couple involves a blended family and the common-law partner with children is receiving child support from the child's biological parent, finances can become more complicated. The parent paying child support does so based on his or her gross annual income. The income of the parent receiving child support is not relevant to the base monthly amount that is paid for child support, nor is the income of a common-law partner relevant to the calculation of child support. We will examine this calculation in more detail in an upcoming chapter, but for now consider the following example:

> Tom and Cindy live common law. Cindy has three children from her first marriage with Gary. Gary has regular access to the children and pays child support to Cindy based on his gross annual income of $144,800 a year. His monthly tax-free payment to Cindy for child support is $2,504 for three children. This is to cover their food, shelter, clothing and other basic needs. Cindy, on the other hand, earns about $130,000 a year and she and Gary split equally all of the other special expenses related to the children's music lessons, dance lessons, and swimming. This has resulted in Gary providing an additional $3,000 per year for the children's extracurricular activities. Gary's total payments to Cindy per year for child support are, therefore, $2,504 per month times 12 months, plus $3,000, for a grand total of $33,048 per year. This money is tax free in Cindy's hands and not deductible to Gary.

How do Tom and Cindy manage Gary's financial contribution to their household? Clearly, with the exception of the special expenses, Gary has no input into how Cindy spends the child support. How does Cindy manage the child support in a way that maximizes the intended benefits to her children? For some families, it may mean something as simple as a deposit of the entire child support directly into a joint account with no discussion about how it is spent. Other families may parse out the child support into RESP accounts, children's savings accounts, or for clothing, allowances, extra-curricular expenses, and so on.

If both common-law partners are receiving child support, allocation can become even more complicated, especially when incomes of the payor spouses (the one paying support) are very different and, therefore, the amounts of child support being paid for the respective children varies widely. Imagine, for example, in the Tom and Cindy scenario, if Tom had three children from his previous relationship and was receiving child support from his previous spouse. If his previous spouse earned $40,400 per year, her contribution for the three children would be $782 per month. In other words, Tom is contributing to the household budget support from his former partner of less than $800 a month for his three children, while Cindy's former partner, Gary, is contributing over $3,000 a month for her three children. It can be tricky ensuring that everyone is treated equally and fairly.

Another common scenario is the situation faced by a common-law couple when one partner is a recipient of child support and one partner is a payor of child support. Consider the following example:

> Phil is separated from Patty and pays her $900 per month for child support for their two children. Phil now lives with Amanda and she receives $900 per month for child support from her former partner, Allan, for their one child. Money flows in and money flows out. Is Allan simply paying Phil's child support obligation to Patty? No, of course not, but it may feel like that. So you can see that child support in blended families can be a source of friction.

As we will see in Chapter 6, many of these issues can be addressed in a cohabitation agreement, but they highlight some of the financial issues faced by common-law couples with blended families (and, of course, it becomes even more complicated if one common-law partner is also receiving spousal support).

WHAT ABOUT PROPERTY?

We do not think of it from day-to-day, but as we acquire property—cars, furniture, electronic entertainment systems, sports equipment, pots and pans and even real estate—there is technical legal ownership of these assets. In other words, a person is "the legal owner" of the item and entitled to have the law support their ownership rights, perhaps by forcing the item of property to be returned or held in safekeeping if taken by a third party. Ownership also entitles a person to pledge the asset as security for a loan. This can range from a form of loan as simple as taking your guitar to a pawnshop to taking out a million-dollar mortgage on a recreational property. Ownership also means the right to sell the object outright. In common-law relationships, couples acquire property in exactly the same way as legally married couples—sometimes one person buys the flat-screen TV and someone else buys the new bicycles or the family car. In some cases, the ownership is joint and both names appear on the ownership, as would be the case with the ownership, for example, of a family home.

In the case of common-law couples, ownership—and more importantly, *proof of ownership*—is very critical. As we will see in the next chapter, in the event of a separation or the death of a common-law spouse, proof of ownership is the starting point for the way in which these couples must separate their property. This means that while it is advisable that all couples maintain records of their finances and acquisition of property, it should be absolutely mandatory for common-law couples to keep such records, as the reliance on this information is very, very important should proof of ownership be needed. Cohabitation agreements work well in this respect because they can provide a starting point for proof or acknowledgement of ownership of property at the outset of a common-law relationship.

WHAT ABOUT INCOME AND EXPENSES?

Again, just as in the case of married couples, common-law couples have a variety of ways of managing their income—joint bank accounts into which all income is deposited, separate bank accounts, a combination of separate and joint. Sometimes, one person manages the finances and sometimes it is shared or alternated (or in some nightmare cases, no one is really taking care of the money). An understanding is reached by the couple about how much it costs to run their household and their respective contributions are made to cover these costs.

In some common-law cases, the couple reaches a very specific arrangement for managing their incomes. Consider, for example, the case where the couple began cohabiting and the husband ran the finances. It was "his house" and they were "his bills" which had to be paid. His common-law partner was required to contribute $575 per month to cover her share of his expenses. A ledger was kept with the heading "Rent." Each month he sat down and recorded her payment at the same time he wrote out cheques to cover utilities and taxes. It didn't matter whether she made $10,000 a year or $500,000 a year, her share of the household expenses was simply $575.

In another case, the couple simply deposited their entire earnings into a joint account and then allocated the balance to various accounts, including his and her RRSPs, RESPs for their children, a vacation account, savings account, debt reduction, and so on. Again, this occurred regardless of their respective earnings. As long as the couple is in agreement, the system works. As long as each person in the couple is employed, the system will work. Just as in the case of an acquisition of a property, record keeping of income and expenses is very important for common-law couples. Again, a cohabitation agreement can work wonders for managing any agreement with respect to income and allocation of expenses.

WHAT ABOUT MEDICAL/DENTAL HEALTH BENEFITS?

Both public and private health plans allow a common-law partner to designate a spouse for the purpose of the plan. The period of cohabitation required in order to qualify varies from plan to plan and can be anywhere from immediate qualification to a requirement of one year of cohabitation. Some plan administrators encounter problems in trying to enforce a qualifying period because, as we saw in the section "When does cohabitation begin?" it can be difficult to establish the starting point.

A common question for common-law couples who want to share a health plan is whether a plan member can have two spouses on the same plan at the same time. Usually, this involves a legally married spouse, from whom he or she is not yet divorced, and a new common-law partner who, together with his or her children, is vying to be on a plan. Plans do not allow this type of double coverage and choices can be difficult. Generally, an existing legally married spouse and children have clear priority. Common-law couples need to check their respective health plans to see what qualifying period, if any, is required to access benefits, and what entitlement there is to benefits for a common-law spouse and stepchildren.

WHAT ABOUT INCOME TAX RETURNS?

If you live common law for at least one year, you are able to use income tax provisions available to spouses. Go to the Canada Revenue Agency's website http://www.cra-arc.gc.ca for exact up-to-date information.

WHAT ABOUT WILLS AND POWERS OF ATTORNEY?

All couples, whether legally married or common law, require wills. If a will is not in place at the time of a person's death, they are considered to have died intestate, and it becomes necessary to use the succession law of the province in which they reside in order to determine how their property will be allocated among surviving family. If a person is legally married, a surviving legal spouse has automatic entitlements under provincial laws (e.g., in Ontario, a surviving legally married spouse receives what is called "the preferential share" before any other beneficiary). Common-law spouses do not automatically have an entitlement to a share of the estate. This has meant that in some cases, when common-law partners died without a will in place, their surviving common-law spouses are left to fight with the deceased's children from previous relationships, previous legally married spouses of the deceased, siblings of the deceased, and even the deceased's parents. All couples need wills, but common-law couples need them more than anyone.

If you die, your property will need to be distributed, your debts paid and, if possible, directions given for your funeral, organ donation and the like. As should be clear from the foregoing sections, clear records of ownership are required, but never more so than for when you are not around to give directions on who gets what and who owns what at the time of your death. We will be looking at the consequences of death for common-law couples in Chapter 5, but at this stage, the key thing to remember is that, as a common-law couple, you need to have wills and powers of attorney in place to manage this critical time.

The same is true with respect to powers of attorney for personal care and property (these documents are known by different names in various provinces. For example, in British Columbia, they are referred to as "mandates"). These documents are legal authority for a person to make decisions on behalf of an individual if they are not in a position to make the decision themselves. Common-law couples require these kinds of powers of attorney if they wish to participate in decision making around property and personal care of their common-law spouse.

~

What have we learned from the topics this chapter has covered?

1. There is great variety in common-law relationships and they cover everything from two young people just starting out living together informally to older people trying common-law as a "post-divorce" or "post-death of a spouse" living arrangement.
2. These relationships often function very much like legal marriages with respect to children, sharing expenses, acquiring property (and debts), sharing medical/dental benefits, income tax consequences, and in experiencing trauma such an injuries, death, and separation.
3. Common-law couples need ways to manage their relationship, perhaps, even more so than legally married couples. Common-law

> couples can benefit from cohabitation agreements, wills, and powers of attorney, particularly if there are children involved.

Let's turn now to a further "reality check" on these relationships and try to answer these questions: What happens if the relationship ends? What if you separate? What if you cannot agree on your rights and obligations to each other? What will the law do—or not do—for you?

4

THE LEGAL CONSEQUENCES OF LIVING COMMON LAW: RIGHTS AND RESPONSIBILITIES IF YOU SEPARATE

The political entities that comprise Canada are the ten provinces, Northwest Territories, Yukon, and Nunavut. Each entity has a different protocol around the legal rights and responsibilities for common-law couples. Before you get too discouraged at the thought of figuring out which laws apply to you and which do not, see the Table of Common Law Rights and Responsibilities in the appendices for an overview. There are a number of common approaches to the issues encountered by common-law couples, such as separation, or the death of a partner. The protocols for custody, access to children, child support and even spousal support all enjoy some uniformity. Property division, on the other hand, differs from province to province and territory. In this chapter, we will examine each of the key areas, look at examples of actual cases, and examine common approaches. But we will also zero in on the specific differences between the treatment of legally married spouses and common-law spouses. The goal is to inform you about what happens to common-law couples who separate and do not have a cohabitation agreement in place. Let's begin with an important question.

WHEN DOES COHABITATION END?

You will recall the discussion of when cohabitation begins in the section When Does Cohabitation Begin? at the opening of Chapter 3. An actual date can be difficult to pin down for some couples. The same can be true for both common-law couples and married couples trying to determine the point of separation. The actual moment of the relationship's end can seem like a moving target. There must be evidence of a desire on behalf of and action by at least one of the parties to terminate it. If the former partners agree that, for example, the big argument they had on New Year's Eve and the fact that one person had moved out is evidence that the relationship was over on January 1, then the actual point of separation will not be difficult to establish. But what if both of them have not applied their minds to the question? What if only one person considers the relationship to be over? What if the other person thinks that, while the relationship is in trouble, counselling may save it? Are they then indeed separated?

Consider the following first interview between a lawyer and a common-law spouse who thinks his relationship has been over for several months:

> "When did you separate?"
>
> "Last summer. The relationship ended completely."
>
> "What happened last summer?"
>
> "We had an argument about whether to have children. When we couldn't agree we stopped having sex, so it was over."
>
> "So the last time the two of you were intimate was last summer?"
>
> "Yes . . . except for her birthday at a friend's cottage and once at Christmas and New Year's Eve, but it really ended last summer when we were both feeling very unhappy."
>
> "When did you tell your family that you were separating?"
>
> "Uh, we didn't."

> "When did you tell your friends?"
>
> "Uh, we didn't."
>
> "Did you tell any of your co-workers?"
>
> "No."
>
> "Is she still on your medical/dental plan?"
>
> "Yes."
>
> "If I asked your neighbours, what would they say?"
>
> "Uh, nothing. They don't know anything about the separation."
>
> "Are you eating meals together, doing your laundry together and so on?"
>
> "Yes but …"
>
> "Does she know you are here?"
>
> "No way."
>
> "If she was sitting here and I asked her what she thinks, what would she say?"
>
> "She would want to work on the relationship by going to counselling."

Does that sound like a real-life situation? Yes. Do they sound like they are separated? No. For more insight, take the list of questions on page 35 in Chapter 3 and reverse them. Separation does not mean that both people need to agree that they are separated. It takes two to begin a relationship, but only one to end it. However, both people must be aware that one of them is actually calling it quits. Consider the following conversation:

> "Sarah, we need to talk about where we are going with this relationship."
>
> "I know where you're going with this. We are not splitting up, Allan."
>
> "I have spoken with a lawyer and …"
>
> "You what?!"

"I have spoken with a lawyer and our relationship is over. I want to have an amicable discussion about what we do next to move on with our lives and still be friends."

"No way, I don't agree."

"I'm sorry."

In the context of a separation conversation, this fits the necessary bill. Both parties are aware and one has acted in a decisive way. If that conversation was confirmed in writing, for example, by email, it would be conclusive proof that the relationship had come to an end.

Now we all know that conversations aren't always that articulate or clear, and some don't occur at all. More often than not the couples allow an unhappy relationship to drift along. They are unhappy, they snipe at each other, intimacy dies; they keep busy and away from each other. They are afraid to confront what needs to be done, and then one person in the relationship does something, consciously or unconsciously, to deal a fatal blow to the relationship—has an affair, begins an abusive argument, or engages in violence or some hurtful or embarrassing behaviour. And then nothing can be said or done to deny that it's over. It is a sad way to end a relationship, and yet this is what happens to many couples.

This is a good opportunity to put to rest a confusing bit of language that lawyers hear from clients: "We're not legally separated." As lawyers, we always scratch our heads and wonder what clients mean by that expression "legally separated." It implies that people could be "illegally" separated. There is no such terminology. You are either separated or not. I think that what clients probably mean is that the relationship is over, but they have not sorted out their legal issues by way of an agreement or a court order.

It is possible to be separated, even though you continue to live under the same roof. Consider the example of the conversation set out above and imagine at the end of it the husband adds, "We cannot afford to separate and live in two apartments right now. Our lease is up in six months, so I think we should give our notice and start looking for new places of our own." If they then continue at the same address until the lease expires, they will still be considered to be separated and the relationship over. There are many cases in which Canadian courts have found a couple to have been separated, even though they continued under the same roof.

We will see in a few minutes why pinpointing this date of separation can be very important to the determination of a division of property, the calculation of spousal support and other issues that need to be addressed when common-law couples split. The importance of the date is the same regardless of where you live—and separate—in Canada.

WHAT HAPPENS IF WE HAVE CHILDREN AND SEPARATE?

Custody and access questions at the time of separation are among the most emotional. If the way in which the relationship ends is painful or unpleasant, it often contaminates the way in which a couple decides to make post-separation decisions about their children.

Consider Jake, age 40, and Renée, age 35. They were together for seven years and have two children who are now six and four. The last year was rough because Renée had been ill. She had just started back to work when she learned that Jake had been having an affair with a sales rep who was a client of his. Renée had been to business dinners with Jake and this young woman, Allison, age 30. Now she feels angry and humiliated. Jake has moved out to live with Allison and her two children, and wants to take his new girlfriend and all of the children on a vacation. As you can well imagine, it may be difficult for Renée and Jake to come to an agreement about custody and access with that kind of context to their relationship breakdown.

If they cannot agree, the court will be forced to step in and make custody and access orders. "Custody" means being given complete care and control of the children, and the equivalent of visiting time to the other parent, called "access." What will the court consider in the circumstances of separation (regardless whether the couple is legally married or common law) in trying to decide what would be appropriate for the children after separation? The court focuses on one overarching goal—protecting the best interests of the children. What factors does it consider when looking at a child's best interests?

Consider the following:

- the relationship between the child and any person claiming custody or access to the child
- the relationship of the child to other members of that family (for example, siblings)
- the child's relationship to other people involved in that child's care and upbringing (for example, day-care workers and grandparents, as well as aunts and uncles)
- the child's views and preferences, provided those views and preferences can be reasonably ascertained (this usually means children who are over the age of 10)
- the length of time the child has lived in a stable home environment
- the ability and willingness of each person seeking custody or access to provide the child with guidance, education and the necessaries of life, or to meet any special needs that the child may have
- proposed plans for the child's care and upbringing
- the ability of a person to act as a parent to this child
- the relationship by blood or through an adoption order between the child and other people involved in the Court Application
- past conduct of a person, if the court is satisfied that the conduct is relevant to that person's ability to act as a parent
- whether the people applying for custody or access have at any time committed violence or abuse against a spouse, a parent, a member of the person's household or the child himself or herself

Unfortunately, parents often do not realize until too late in the proceedings that a court is not particularly interested in behaviour that does not affect the ability to parent. So, for example, Jake's affair with Allison has absolutely nothing to do with his ability to parent the two children involved. If the situation involves a blended family, the court will be concerned with maintaining a relationship between the biological child and parent. However, there is no automatic entitlement to custody, and the courts have been prepared to award custody of a child to a non-biological step-parent if the biological parent is unable to look after the child's best interests. At the very least, a step-parent does have an opportunity to ask for access to the children post separation.

At the conclusion of findings to these enquiries, which may be assisted by third-party investigators (such as social workers, private assessors, psychiatrists, psychologists, lawyers for the children, and even Children's Aid Societies), a determination is made that is presumably in the best interests of the children. These third-party investigations (which may cost thousands of dollars) will examine everything from relationships with grandparents, the child's education and school experience, the child's circle of friends, sports and hobbies, and other extracurricular activities, and then compare how each parent participates in those aspects of the child's life. A report is prepared with recommendations that the court should try to "preserve the child's universe" as much as possible.

The court has some limited options available to it when dealing with custody of children. In some cases parents agree that one parent should have custody and the other should have access. But more modern families, where both parents have been involved with the children's upbringing, often use concepts such as joint custody, shared parenting, or parallel parenting to manage the care of the children after separation.

In the case of joint custody, the parents share time with the children and responsibilities for their upbringing. The same is true with shared parenting, where the parents co-operate, in some cases simply replicating what they did while together but from separate houses. The mother will look after getting the children to medical and dental appointments and the father will look after getting them to their recreational activities and music lessons. Parallel parenting has been a relatively recent development. It involves parents who have difficulty communicating with each other, but are prepared to try to parent their children in the absence of any direct parental co-operation. This means that in the mother's home a set of rules is developed, the children abide by those rules and the mother accepts certain responsibilities while the children are with her. The children then move to the father's home, where the father has a set of rules (which we hope are at least similar to the mother's). The father then takes responsibility for the children while they are with him. While this form of parallel parenting continues, the parents do not communicate with each other. Each of the above options is available to common-law parents.

Other issues that need to be sorted out after separation include developing a schedule of time for the children to be with each parent, which can be complicated, depending on where the parents live. Mobility rights are also an issue because Canadian parents move within Canada and abroad. The ability of a parent to move with the children in such a way that interferes with the other parent's time with the children is very restricted in Canada. Another issue that involves careful balancing between households is managing the religious practices of the children. This can include a parent insisting on a particular religious upbringing or, alternatively, a parent insisting on no religious training in their upbringing.

The bottom line is that if you live in a common-law relationship and have children, or have blended children into a new family, and you then separate and you are unable to agree on a post-separation, custody-access arrangement, a court will examine the best interests of your children and then grant one parent custody, the other parent access, or employ one of the other options of joint custody, shared parenting, or parallel parenting, and apportion rights and responsibilities for the children accordingly. In this regard, common-law parents are treated exactly the same way as legally married parents.*

WHAT HAPPENS IF WE HAVE CHILDREN WHO NEED FINANCIAL SUPPORT?

Provisions regarding financial support for children are uniform for common-law spouses and married parents due to the implementation in 1997 of the Child Support Guidelines. The Child Support Guidelines have the force of federal and provincial law by virtue of some amendments to the federal *Divorce Act* and provincial family laws. Related amendments were also made at the same time to the *Income Tax Act*.

The Child Support Guidelines were updated in May of 2006 and the impact of the guidelines has been to bring a great deal of predictability to the area of family law. These guidelines ensure fairness and consistency in the amount of child support. They also reduce the

---

* For more information on this topic see my book *Surviving Your Divorce: A Guide to Canadian Family Law*, 4th edition.

likelihood of conflict between parents and lawyers arguing over how much child support is appropriate. The Guidelines provide a faster and less costly way of resolving the issue of child support when families separate. It was also the Guidelines that converted the approach to child support from one of income tax deductibility to net amounts. Once the amount of child support is calculated, it is paid to a recipient parent who does not include it in their income, and neither does the paying parent deduct it from his or her income. It is net after-tax dollars flowing from household to household.

The application of the Child Support Guidelines formula involves the use of tables that establish monthly amounts for child support based on the number of children in question and the paying spouse's gross annual income. For the tables to apply, one parent must be the custodial parent or the parent who has primary residence for the children. This would generally mean that the other parent has the children 40 percent or less of the time. In many cases, however, children reside with one parent for at least 65 percent or 70 percent of the time. The access parent may be seeing the children every second weekend and perhaps one overnight visit in alternate weeks. Vacation time and holidays are split equitably between the parents or in such a way that allows the accommodation of their own vacation schedules.

Child support, then, falls into two categories: a base monthly amount of child support and a sharing of special expenses for the children. In the calculation of the base monthly child support, the annual income of the custodial parent is not taken into account. The guidelines focus on the gross annual income of the non-custodial parent. Lawyers have software programs that calculate the amount of support and it is possible to go to the federal Department of Justice website (www.justice.gc.ca/eng/index) and do the calculation online.

Each province has its own version of the Guidelines for application to provincial support orders, and these Guidelines govern common-law couples. They are designed and tailored to each province's respective standard and cost of living. This means that a person paying child support in Ontario will have a slightly different figure on a monthly basis than a person paying child support in Nova Scotia, even though they may have the same gross annual income.

~

In applying the Guidelines, six questions are posed:

1. How many children are involved?
2. What is the custody arrangement?
3. What is the annual income of the paying parent?
4. What does the table in the Guidelines set out as the amount?
5. Are there any extraordinary or special expenses for the children?
6. Will there be undue hardship if the Child Support Guidelines are used in the particular circumstances of this case?

An example of the application of the Child Support Guidelines would be as follows: Let's assume that a mother and father have separated and there are three children and that the father earns $81,900 per year. His child support obligation would be $1,541 per month for the three children.

The foregoing monthly amount of support, called the base amount of support, is supposed to assist a parent with the cost of housing, clothing, feeding and meeting the miscellaneous day-to-day expenses of the children. Over and above that base amount, both the custodial and non-custodial parents also contribute to what are called "special or extraordinary expenses" related to the children. They should consult each other prior to incurring these expenses and then divide them in proportion to their annual incomes. So, for example, if a child is a talented figure skater and requires special lessons, and custom skates and must travel to competitive events, this would likely be considered an expense over and above the base amount incurred each month for that child by the custodial parent. The parents would typically consult with each other, agree on the incurring of the special expense and then divide it in proportion to their annual incomes. There is no fixed list of special expenses because these types of things vary from family to family, but consider some of the following possible special expenses:

- childcare expenses incurred as a result of a custodial parent's employment, illness, disability or education, or training for employment
- that portion of medical and dental insurance premiums attributed to the child
- health-related expenses that exceed insurance reimbursement for the child's treatment for orthotics, professional counselling, social

workers, psychiatrists, physiotherapy, speech therapy, hearing aids, glasses and contact lenses
- extraordinary expenses for primary or secondary school education or for any other educational programs that meet the child's particular needs
- expenses for post-secondary education including residence, tuition, books and even a new computer
- extraordinary expenses for special extra curricular activities such as sports or music
- the most frequent special expense—braces

These types of expenses are supposed to be reasonable in the context of the particular family. Generally, the higher the level of income, the more extensive the availability of special expenses for the children. For example, private school might be considered an appropriate special expense for a particular family, if the incomes are high. On the other hand, in a Saskatchewan case, the court ruled that piano lessons were too expensive for the particular family in question.

As the parents' incomes may increase or decline, the amount of child support changes. This is usually calculated on an annual basis based on income tax returns and Notices of Assessment. It can sometimes be an open question about when the child support should end. If a child turns 18 and is no longer in school, child support will end generally. If a child continues in school, then the child support may continue until that child is in his or her early twenties. If a child has special medical needs or is, for example, suffering from a disability the child support can continue indefinitely.

One issue that arises in common-law cases involving blended families is the obligation of a step-parent for child support after the separation. In such cases, the court attempts to determine whether a step-parent has acted as if he or she was the child's parent (called *loco parentis*), even though they are not the biological or adoptive parent. The court will ask questions such as:

- Did this person provide a large part of the financial support necessary for the child?
- Did the person intend to step into the shoes of a parent?
- Was the relationship between the person and the child a continuing one with some permanency?

- Can inferences be drawn from the treatment the child would receive were he or she living with their biological parent?
- Has the person ceased to act as a parent of that child?

The court also looks at such things as the affection between the person and child, the length of time of the association and whether the child has taken the surname of that step-parent and lives in the same dwelling.

The Child Support Guidelines even deal with such things as split custody (where one child goes to live with one parent and another child goes to live with the other parent), situations where there is more than one parent obligated to pay child support, situations of financial hardship, and situations where the noncustodial parent sees the child more than 40 percent of the time (and the Guidelines therefore don't apply). All of these things have an impact on the calculation of the amount of child support.

The bottom line for child support is that if you separate from a common-law relationship, the Child Support Guidelines will supply a reliable method of calculating child support, extending as far as the children complete university.

WHAT HAPPENS TO PROPERTY THAT WE OWNED BEFORE WE BEGAN LIVING TOGETHER?

As a general rule, any property brought into a common-law relationship will leave with its owner: a vehicle, furniture, sports equipment, pensions, savings, real estate, and even a business. Ownership follows the legal title.

The exception to this general rule concerns the situation that occurs all too often in common-law relationships with respect to real estate and businesses in particular—both spouses treat the property in the name of one spouse as if it was owned by both. They inhabit and work on the property, invest in the business, provide services in the home, but one spouse does not have his or her name as a legal owner. In this section I would like to take a look at some examples of situations into which common-law spouses have fallen and examine how Canadian courts developed a number of legal tools to assist them.

The starting point is a case involving the woman I mentioned in the acknowledgements of this book, Ms. Rosa Becker. Her case went all the way to the Supreme Court of Canada and she was successful to a certain extent—she got a favourable judgement but she was never able to collect all of the money that was owed to her. Feeling helpless and defeated by the system, she killed herself in protest over the way in which she had been treated. Her tragic life has always stuck with me and I think consideration of her case provides insight into the predicament of common-law spouses.

Mr. Pettkus and Ms. Becker emigrated to Canada from Central Europe in the early 1950s. Like many immigrants, they had a few dollars in their pockets when they arrived and set out to work hard in their new country. When they met in Montreal, Ms. Becker was 30 years of age and Mr. Pettkus was 25. After a while, they began to live together and within a few years he was introducing her as his wife. He even took the step of claiming her as a spouse for income tax purposes.

Over the years they worked and led a hardscrabble life, with Mr. Pettkus repairing and restoring motor vehicles and Ms. Becker taking a variety of menial jobs. Her income paid the expenses and he banked up to $12,000 by 1960, a considerable achievement, considering they had just arrived in Canada. They travelled to Western Canada, sharing expenses, scouting for a suitable farm location upon which they could start a beekeeping business. Ultimately, they returned to Eastern Canada, buying a farm in Quebec with Mr. Pettkus' savings. Title was taken in his name alone. However, when the farmhouse needed repairs to the floor and roof, it was Ms. Becker who used her money to buy the materials and actually assist in doing the work of laying the floor and installing a bathroom.

Their beekeeping business was established and both of them worked hard at it, making frames for the hives, moving the bees to orchards of neighbouring farmers, checking the hives, and extracting the honey in late summer. They expanded the business and bought property in Ontario, again with money that had been saved by Mr. Pettkus, and again with title taken in his name alone. After further acquisitions of property and expansion of their beekeeping business, the relationship began to deteriorate. There was one break-up and then a reconciliation, but by 1974 they had ended it. She left with a 1966

Volkswagen and $2,600 in cash. She sued for a fair share and, in 1980, the Supreme Court came to the conclusion that Mr. Pettkus was able to purchase a farm and operate a beekeeping business because he had received the benefit of 19 years of unpaid labour from Ms. Becker. She had received little or nothing in return. The court stated that common-law couples could be compensated for their work through the use of a legal tool known as a constructive trust. In other words, the party who has title to the property holds a part of it in trust for the party whose name is not on it. In order to come to a conclusion that a constructive trust should be used, three requirements must be satisfied:

1. There must be an enrichment of one spouse.
2. There must be a corresponding deprivation for the other spouse.
3. There must be an absence of any legal reason for one spouse to be enriched at the other's expense.

Ms. Becker was successful, and though she never collected, she broke legal ground for common-law spouses across Canada.

Other cases followed her and, in the next section, I will set out some examples of situations into which common-law couples across Canada have fallen, situations such as these:

- A man and a woman lived together for 42 years. In addition to doing all of the household work and raising six children, the common-law wife worked on a farm that was owned by her common-law husband. The court found that the husband clearly derived a benefit from the wife's many years of labour in the home and on the farm. The benefit included valuable financial savings from his having had work on the farm and work in the home performed by the wife and not having had to pay for it.
- In an Ontario case, the common-law husband owned shares in a family business. The wife made significant contributions to the success of the business and even mortgaged her interest in the matrimonial home to protect his investment in the business. She also worked in various aspects of the business over the years without compensation. The court found that the husband had been unjustly enriched at her expense and gave her a 25-percent interest in the common shares of the company.

- In a B.C. case, the common-law wife invested labour and money in a home that was registered in the husband's name. They lived frugally and, as a result, the husband was able to build up his RRSPs for retirement. When they separated after 17 years of cohabitation, the court did not think it was fair that she should leave the relationship with nothing. A constructive trust was imposed on the assets owned by the husband.
- In an Ontario case, the common-law wife's housekeeping and childcare duties, which were delivered without compensation, allowed the husband to pay off a mortgage on property that he owned and to purchase other assets. In such circumstances, the court considered a constructive trust an appropriate way of protecting the wife's interests.
- In a B.C. case, the common-law husband paid for a house and the renovations to it, but the wife assisted with the renovations and was in attendance during virtually all of the construction. This meant that the common-law husband was free to work on other matters. In addition, the common-law wife undertook domestic duties, including entertaining and housekeeping and providing the husband with several months of care when he was ill. She was not compensated for any of the assistance she gave and the court found that the intensity of her contribution over a short period of time—fewer than three years—still created a situation of unjust enrichment if the husband was left with all of the assets and she was left with none.
- In a B.C. case, a couple had lived together for 16 years. The common-law wife was employed full-time as a geologist throughout the relationship while the husband had a Grade 12 education and no other training. He stayed home and did the housework while she pursued her career. In addition, he did repairs and renovations on the home and the court found that he should be compensated for the work that was done in the relationship. A constructive trust was used.
- In an Alberta case, the husband and wife cohabited in the husband's residence for approximately eight years. During that time, the wife worked in his business as a bookkeeper. However, she did receive a wage for that work, unlike the work that she did in the

> home as the primary homemaker, gardener, and contributor to household expenses. By the time they separated, the common-law wife was on social assistance, while the common-law husband's assets had increased in value significantly. The court had little difficulty finding a way to compensate her through a constructive trust.

Once the court developed a legal tool that would assist common-law spouses, a debate emerged over how to value the contribution that was to be compensated. Two approaches have been used, known as either the "value received approach" or the "value survived approach." In a "value received approach," the court looks to see what services were provided by each spouse within the relationship and then attempts to find a way to compensate the spouse who was unjustly enriched. In the "value survived approach," the court looks at the value of property brought into the relationship, the value of property acquired during the relationship and then examines the increase in the value of those assets at the end of the relationship. In some cases, the courts have blurred the two approaches and considered both the services that were delivered and the value of assets that were acquired.

In a recent Ontario case, the Ontario Court of Appeal confirmed that the correct approach, at least for Ontario cases, is to calculate the value received and ensure that each party is fairly compensated. In that case, the common-law husband and wife had lived together for approximately 12 years. They had two children when the relationship ended. Over the course of the relationship, the husband had developed a network operating system company and the other spouse was employed by CSIS. The couple had moved from Ontario to Nova Scotia and then returned to Ontario. The trial judge concluded that the common-law husband could not have built up the company without the efforts of his common-law wife supporting him. When that company was ultimately sold and the husband retired, he received approximately $11,000,000 from the sale of the company shares. It had to be shared.

This same issue of how to calculate the value of the unjust enrichment has been tackled in cases across Canada. In one B.C. case, the British Columbia Court of Appeal stated that, "Long-term marriage-like relationships will usually require the use of the 'value survived approach,' not only because contributions to such partnerships neither can or should be measured with precision, but also because such an approach is seen as according with the expectations of both parties in such a relationship, barring evidence of a contrary understanding." The court in that case felt that there was no universally correct method of ascertaining the value of a constructive trust. When one considers cases across the country, it appears that the value survived approach is the usual response. It has been said that one of the reasons the courts rely on the value survived approach is that there is difficulty in attempting to place a value on services performed.

However, the bottom line is that property owned before the relationship will remain with that owner after the relationship ends, unless the other spouse invested labour and/or money into the property for which a court thinks they deserve compensation. In that case, the court will calculate the value of that work and order compensation to the spouse. The property will still remain with the legal owner, but compensation will flow to the other spouse.

We will see how to manage such issues in Chapter 6, "Creating Your Own Set of Rights and Responsibilities." In that chapter, we will set out methods for avoiding confusion, as well as expensive and often acrimonious disputes like those set out above.

WHAT HAPPENS TO PROPERTY WE ACQUIRED WHILE TOGETHER?

Property acquired in both names will be divided equally between common-law spouses, unless there is a good reason to divide it otherwise than equally together. However, it is in this discussion of property division that the approach changes from province to province and territories. Let's start by considering the approach used in several provinces (for example, Ontario, British Columbia, New Brunswick).

In Ontario, common-law spouses have no statutory property rights. None. The only entitlement is as might be established using the approach and tools described in the previous section—unjust enrichment, constructive trust and *quantum meruit*. If one spouse puts his or her money in RRSPs, then they will leave with those savings. If she or he chooses to save their money by investing in stocks and bonds or precious metals, then they will keep those assets. If one spouse acquired property, such as real estate or a business, during the course of the relationship and the other spouse, even though they had no legal title to the property, invested their time and labour in the asset, the same approaches and tools will be used to provide that spouse with a fair share of the increase in value attributable to their work or investment.

The discussion in the previous section about constructive trusts, unjust enrichment, and the value received and value survived approaches applies equally to property that is acquired in the name of one spouse after the cohabitation begins. Cases across Canada have required the court to look at property acquired both before and after the relationship began to see if one party's contribution through finances, through labour, through childcare, or other services should be compensated. In order to use a constructive trust as a tool to assist a common-law spouse, the court must find that there has been an unjust enrichment, and that requires (1) an enrichment, (2) a corresponding deprivation, and (3) an absence of any legal reason for one spouse to be enriched at the expense of the other.

In Manitoba and Nova Scotia, there are laws that allow common-law couples to register their relationships with the provincial government. By doing so they gain extra rights and privileges. In some cases, by registering they are treated as if they are legally married. Registration is voluntary. In others, it may eliminate the need for a cohabitation agreement or to complement an agreement.

For Manitoba see www.gov.mb.ca/justice/family/law or call 1-800-282-8069, ext 3701.

For Nova Scotia see www.gov.ns.ca/just/flic. I do not foresee this system of registering domestic partnerships spreading to other provinces in the future.

WHAT IF ONE OF US NEEDS FINANCIAL SUPPORT AFTER SEPARATION?

If you meet your provincial/territorial standard for becoming a common-law spouse, any entitlement to spousal support will be calculated in exactly the same way as a legally married couple. Let's look at the approaches used by Canadian courts. (In Appendix D I have provided a table that shows the way in which an entitlement for spousal support arises in each Canadian province and territory.)

When making spousal support orders, the court tries to do a number of things:

1. Recognize any economic advantages or disadvantages to the spouses arising from the relationship or its breakdown;
2. Apportion between the spouses the financial consequences arising from the care of children;
3. Relieve any economic hardship of the spouses arising from the breakdown of the relationship;
4. Promote the economic self-sufficiency of each spouse within a reasonable period of time.

In making support orders, the court considers certain factors including the condition, means, needs, and other circumstances of each spouse. This will include looking at the length of time the spouses cohabited, the functions performed by the spouses during the cohabitation, and any other factor relevant to the support of a spouse.

Spousal support is generally ordered to be paid on a periodic basis (e.g., a monthly payment of a fixed sum directly from one spouse to the other). The spouse who receives the spousal support payment must include it in his or her income and pay tax on it. The spouse who pays the spousal support deducts it on his or her income tax return.

In calculating spousal support the court focuses on the spouse's needs and the other spouse's ability to pay. Much can depend on the nature of the relationship, but generally a dependent spouse is entitled to a standard of living that is equal to or near what he or she could have expected. Entitlement, quantum, and duration will vary from couple to couple.

A recent development with respect to spousal support was the development of the Spousal Support Advisory Guidelines. Technically, these guidelines are not law in the same sense as the Child Support Guidelines, but they are an attempt to bring some predictability and uniformity to the calculation of spousal support orders across Canada. Some provinces/territories have adopted the Spousal Support Advisory Guidelines more than others. In Ontario, for example, the Spousal Support Advisory Guidelines are, as a result of a decision of the Ontario Court of Appeal, a starting point for the calculation of spousal support in all cases. In order to do a Spousal Support Advisory Guideline calculation, a software program is required. Most family law lawyers now have this software and use the program to calculate spousal support in one of two scenarios:

- separating families where there are children and child support is also being paid;
- separating families where there is no child support.

The SSAGs call for information such as the length of the relationship, the age of the spouses, and any special considerations such as their ability to work and contribute to their own support or conversely their inability to do so because of illness. Once the information has been plugged into the guidelines, two pieces of information are generated: first, a range of quantum of support which might be applicable to the case. This range might provide, for example, that spousal support should be paid in the amount of between $5,000 and $7,500 per month. Second, the guidelines will suggest a term for the payment of the support. In the case of a long relationship of, say, in excess of 20 years, the spousal support will likely be indefinite. In shorter relationships the support may only be for a few years at which time it would end.

Spousal support awards are among the most controversial and emotional issues at the time of separation. In some cases the value of the spousal support award exceeds the property that is being divided between the couple. A spousal support order of $5,000 or $6,000 a month for a 10-year period has a value of hundreds of thousands of dollars. For this reason, when common-law couples separate, this issue can increase acrimony. Clients zero in very quickly on whether they have a spousal support obligation, how much that obligation will be on a monthly basis and when the obligation will end. In this last respect, spousal support obligations do not automatically end when the recipient spouse cohabits with or even marries a new partner. Remarriage or cohabitation may be a set of circumstances that triggers a review of the entitlement or the quantum of spousal support. This, you can well imagine, comes as a painful shock to many separating couples, particularly since Canadians for the most part are not aware of the creation of these rights and responsibilities as they cohabit.

Once again, as should be clear from previous sections of this book, this potential financial obligation can be managed through the terms of a cohabitation agreement.

WHAT IF WE MOVE WHILE LIVING COMMON LAW?

Canadians are mobile, moving from province to province and around the world. Where they ultimately settle is where their legal disputes must be resolved. So, if a common-law couple moves from New Brunswick to Saskatchewan and then separates, or if one of them dies, that is where their legal dispute will be considered through an application of Saskatchewan law. It is therefore possible to move from one type of common-law rights and responsibilities to a completely different set of laws, thereby gaining or losing rights in the process. For example, if a common-law couple lived together for two years in Nova Scotia and met its legal requirement for, say, spousal support, but then moves to Ontario and separates in a province that considers three years of cohabitation as a requirement to qualify for spousal support, then a right to spousal support will have been negated. In the opposite case, a couple may find themselves covered by common-law rights and responsibilities that were never anticipated. For this reason, couples who are living common law must be aware of their potential change in status as they move in Canada and around the world.

As we will see in Chapter 6, this issue can easily be addressed in a cohabitation agreement by stipulating which province or which country's laws and rules will govern the relationship, regardless of where the couple resides.

ARE THERE TIME LIMITS FOR BRINGING A CLAIM?

Custody and access issues are never governed by any time limits. The Court will always be prepared to act to protect the best interests of children. Spousal support claims are best advanced within two years of separation (or immediately, if the need has arisen because of the death of a spouse). After two years, a court may still be prepared to consider a spousal support claim, but questions will arise about the reasons for the delay and what had happened to the spouse in the interim. How, for example, did a spouse support themselves for that period? Were they incapable of advancing a claim due to illness? The same is true for property claims. Too long of a delay may undermine the ability to make a claim against the property. A local lawyer should be consulted about time limits on spousal support and property claims in the province or territory in which the common-law couple resides at the time of separation. As a general rule, remember—delay can be deadly to a claim. So, act quickly to get advice.

~

Now we know what will happen if you live common law without a cohabitation agreement. Custody of or access to children will be determined on their best interests. Child support will be calculated based on the Child Support Guidelines, which are, in turn, based upon the couple's respective gross annual incomes. Spousal support will be calculated in accordance with the Spousal Support Advisory Guidelines or on a variety of factors which basically boil down the needs of one spouse and the ability of the other spouse to pay. Property division will depend on the province in which you reside. Spouses will keep property they brought into the relationship and property that is in their name and acquired during the relationship. Joint property will be divided either equally or in proportion to the contribution made by respective spouses.

However, problems will undoubtedly arise where assets have been blended together or where a spouse has made a financial or labour contribution to the other spouse's property. As a common-law couple, you will need to be aware of the need for record keeping throughout the relationship and be constantly alive to changing rights and responsibilities should you move from province to province or out of the country. Should problems arise in the relationship, there will be a need to establish not only the day upon which the relationship began in its common-law form, but also there will be a need to establish a clear date of separation. These are the things that may happen if you don't have a cohabitation agreement. Now, let's turn to examine what happens if one of you is injured, becomes ill, or dies.

5

THE LEGAL CONSEQUENCES OF LIVING COMMON LAW

RIGHTS AND RESPONSIBILITIES IF ONE OF YOU DIES, IS INJURED, OR BECOMES ILL

Many couples must face something even more frightening than separation—catastrophic injury, illness, and even death of their partner. When these challenges arise, their rights and responsibilities as common-law partners may be brought into very sharp focus. As we saw in Chapter 3, in the section What about Wills and Powers of Attorney?, couples can address the possibility of these challenges with Powers of Attorney for Personal Care, Powers of Attorney for Property, wills, and even through a cohabitation agreement. But what if these documents are not in place? What happens when someone gets very sick, is seriously injured, or dies?

Some Common Scenarios

1. Megan and David have been living together for four years. They have two children and are living in a home owned in David's name

alone. On this particular weekend, David suffers a head injury while biking and is in a coma. Will Megan be able to make decisions to help David while he is in a coma? What about their home and bank accounts? What about his personal care while in hospital?

2. Elana and Sebastian have been living together for six years in a home that is registered in Elana's name alone. They have a joint bank account and they run a bed and breakfast together. This morning, while driving to work, Elana was killed in a car accident. Her will, made ten years ago, leaves everything to her sister. Will Sebastian have any rights to share in Elana's estate? Will her sister get everything?
3. Shawn and Valda have been living together for ten years, but Shawn is still legally married to Alicia and never signed a separation agreement. He dies without a will. Will Valda or Alicia be entitled to Shawn's estate?
4. Elizabeth and Joel have only been living together for a year, but they keep all their money in one joint account. Joel dies suddenly, but leaves a will that doesn't mention Elizabeth. Should Elizabeth keep all the money in the joint account or should Joel's "share" be turned over to his estate to be shared with other beneficiaries?

These are typical questions faced by common-law couples every day. A note of caution is warranted before we go deeper into the discussion: laws governing common-law couples differ between provinces and territories. The examples I use in this chapter are designed to demonstrate what happens in most provinces. In provinces such as Saskatchewan, Manitoba, and Nova Scotia, common-law spouses have more specific rights at the time of death of a spouse. So remember: always check with a local lawyer. Also, see the "Table of Common-Law Rights and Responsibilities" in the appendices. For now, let's look at each challenge.

Joint Property

If a common-law couple owns real property jointly and then one of them dies, the deceased's interest in the property is automatically transferred to the surviving spouse. This transfer occurs by virtue of what is called the "rule of survivorship." The surviving spouse does not need to do anything and the deceased's interest in the property does not even pass through or form a part of his or her estate. It is an excellent method for people to pass on property upon death.

If the couple owns a property together but the title is not held jointly, then it is held as "tenants in common." This means that, if either spouse dies, their interest in the property will flow into their estate and be shared by beneficiaries generally or someone specific if the deceased names a particular person to receive his or her interest in the property. Similarly, if the property is held as tenants in common and the deceased does not have a will, then an intestacy will apply and all property will flow into the hands of someone appointed to administer the estate. Surviving spouses and other family members will then get in line of see if they will share in the estate.

Look again at examples 2 and 3 above. In the case of example 2, Elana's will prevails and her sister will inherit everything. However, if Elana and Sebastian had held the property as joint tenants, Sebastian would have received the home outright and the sister would have received the balance of the estate. If Sebastian and Elana had held the home as tenants in common, Sebastian would have received half and Elana's half would have gone into her estate for her sister.

In the case of example 3, Shawn died intestate and his legal surviving spouse Alicia will be entitled to a preferential share of his estate as will any of his children. In most provinces in Canada (see table in appendices), Valda would receive nothing from the property in his estate. (She could try to sue for support from the estate and she could try to sue asking for a fair share of his property based on her financial or labour contribution of the property, but that is an uphill battle.) Again, had Shawn and Valda held the property as joint tenants or tenants in common, Valda would have had a much greater entitlement.

Joint Accounts

In examples 1 and 4, spouses Megan and Elizabeth will be trying to deal with bank accounts. In Megan's case, David is in a coma. If he has left a Power of Attorney for Property (naming her), then Megan will have no difficulty making decisions to help him, herself, and the children while he is the coma. If he has not left a Power of Attorney for

Property, then the only money that Megan will be able to access immediately is her own bank accounts and any funds that may have been held with David in a joint account. If David had complete control of the bank accounts, then Megan will have a problem, as a common-law spouse will not be able to access his accounts.

In the case of Elizabeth, her problem will be establishing an entitlement to all or even half of the funds in the joint account she held with Joel. Joel did leave a will, so the beneficiaries of Joel's estate will insist that all money in the joint account be returned to his estate and shared by all of his beneficiaries. Technically (at least in the eyes of the Canada Revenue Agency, for example), the funds remaining in the account are Elizabeth's. However, if Joel left some evidence of his intention with respect to this account, then that will be determinative of the account status. Canadian courts have said recently that specific evidence of the deceased's intentions with respect to a joint account is important. Even a letter setting out the deceased person's intention (perhaps kept with the will or with the power of attorney) will be satisfactory. In the absence of such evidence the court will be more likely to assume that a surviving wife or child whose name is on a joint account is supposed to receive the funds in the account outright.

One other issue that Elizabeth will face, of course, is that having only resided with Joel for one year, she may have trouble even establishing that she is a common-law spouse with an entitlement to support from the estate. For example, in Ontario she would not meet the requirement of three years of continuous cohabitation.

Having a Will and Not Having a Will

As we saw in Chapter 4, common-law couples in Canada, for the most part do not have statutory rights to share property should they separate. They are left to gather evidence and to try to prove to a court that the value of property in which they invested money or their labour should be shared. They must sue their spouse to prove a constructive trust or unjust enrichment. The same is true if their spouse has died and left a will that bequeaths their property to someone else, or if they died intestate. The surviving common-law spouse must sue to establish an entitlement to any property that is not in their name. Let's consider four scenarios.

1. The deceased leaves a will in which he leaves everything to his or her common-law spouse.

In a perfect world this is the ideal situation. The deceased looked at his or her property, made a plan and implemented it through a will. A potential problem with such an approach is the possibility that the deceased has a surviving legal spouse from whom he or she is not yet legally divorced. In such a case, and assuming the surviving legally married spouse has unresolved property claims from the marriage, that person has a choice. He or she may take what has been given to them in the deceased's will (in this example nothing), or may take what he or she would have received had they divorced. In other words, even though the entire estate has been left to the common-law spouse, the surviving legally married spouse may still get some of the deceased's property. This means that, for common-law couples, it is not only important to make the will properly with respect to the common-law spouse, but to also ensure that previous marital obligations have been resolved.

2. The deceased leaves a will, leaving everything to a third party (for example, his children from a first marriage) but nothing to the surviving common-law spouse.

In this situation we see the challenge faced by a common-law spouse who has been left nothing by her partner. This can arise in two situations: first, the deceased may have sat down and applied his or her mind to the distribution of property and consciously excluded his or her common-law spouse; alternatively, the will may be old and predated their cohabitation. In either event, what can be done? Again, the only recourse with respect to property division is for the common-law spouse to sue the estate and hope to be able to establish a constructive trust or unjust enrichment based on financial or labour contributions to property not in the surviving spouse's name. And again, if a surviving legal spouse was still in the picture, then the same approach as described in the previous scenario would apply.

3. The deceased leaves no will but has a legally married spouse from whom he or she was not divorced.

In this situation the surviving legally married spouse will have first entitlement to the estate. An administrator for the estate will need to be appointed and the surviving legally married spouse will be first in line to be appointed. A surviving common-law spouse will be litigating with the estate administrator if any share of the property is to be recovered.

4. The deceased leaves no will and has no surviving legally married spouse, but does have a common-law spouse and children from a previous marriage.
In this scenario, the common-law spouse will be disappointed again as the children from a first marriage will have legal priority to the deceased's estate. He or she will be left to litigate to get a fair share of property that is not in their name.

POWERS OF ATTORNEY FOR PERSONAL CARE AND PROPERTY

For common-law couples, these two documents are just as important as wills. A Power of Attorney for Property is designed to appoint someone to make decisions with respect to property in the event the individual making the power of attorney cannot (e.g., if they are in a coma). Without a power of attorney, minimal decisions can be made on behalf of the incapacitated person. Court-ordered authority will be required for anything significant such as dealing with real estate or other significant assets. The same is true for a Power of Attorney for Personal Care, which allows an individual appointed to make decisions related to health and general welfare when the person appointing the attorney cannot make the decision for themselves.

Common-law spouses who find themselves in emergency situations when their spouse is unable to make a decision with respect to their property or with respect to their own care will be frustrated in their attempts to direct financial institutions, health-care providers and other third parties. Powers of Attorney for Personal Care and Property are therefore mandatory. It is for this reason that I urge couples who are considering cohabitation agreements to use that opportunity to discuss and prepare these other supporting documents; they need to discuss their wills, their powers of attorney, and even letters of intent with respect to joint accounts.

SUPPORT

While I have touched on this entitlement in Chapter 4, one of the legal consequences that arises upon the death of a common-law spouse is the possibility of the surviving common-law spouse being dependent and needing to sue the deceased's estate for support. Every province and territory permits a surviving common-law spouse to sue the estate of a deceased spouse for support. In Ontario, for example, Section 58 of the *Succession Law Reform Act*, provides that when a deceased person (whether they died with or without a will) did not make adequate provision for the proper support for his or her dependents, the court may order adequate provision for that individual out of the estate.

Potential dependents include the following:

- a spouse, which includes a common-law spouse or a legally married spouse
- a parent of the deceased, which includes a grandparent or a step-parent
- a child of the deceased
- a brother or sister of the deceased

If any individual in the foregoing categories was dependent upon the deceased (in other words the deceased was providing support to them or was under a legal obligation to provide support to them immediately before his or death), then they may sue the estate for financial assistance. Unfortunately, this type of claim by common-law couples may be their last resort when they have been left high and dry by a deceased common-law spouse.

In addition, there is some pressure to commence such a claim for support in a timely way. In Ontario, for example, a claim by a dependent must be launched within six months of the court granting letters probate of the will (in other words accepting it as a legitimate will) or letters of administration in the case of an intestacy. This means a grieving partner must act quickly.

As we will see in the next chapter ("Creating Your Own Set of Rights and Obligations"), a cohabitation agreement may set out a couple's respective rights and obligations during cohabitation, in the event of a separation, or on death, including ownership in or division of property, support obligations, or any other matter related to the settlement of their affairs. This means that cohabitation agreements are not only of assistance in setting out your rights and obligations while you were together or if you separate, but they can also help in the case of death of a common-law couple.

~

Now you are aware of the consequences of living common law and having to deal with illness, injury, or the death of a partner. Wills, powers of attorney, and statements about intention are critical for common-law couples, especially if they don't have a cohabitation agreement.

6

CREATING YOUR OWN SET OF RIGHTS AND OBLIGATIONS

AN OVERVIEW OF A COHABITATION AGREEMENT

In the previous chapters we have examined the consequences of cohabitation, the rights and responsibilities which arise at the point of separation or if one spouse dies. A cohabitation agreement offers a couple an opportunity to say, "We don't think those rights and responsibilities suit our relationship; we want to tailor our own set of rules; we want to avoid possible confusion and arguments."

The couple may craft this agreement before they cohabit, before any rights and responsibilities have taken hold (and as we have seen that varies from province to province), or after the relationship has been underway for some time. Imagine a contract that provides exactly what you as a couple want in your life, rather than the anxiety and uncertainty that can corrode a relationship.

In Chapter 11, "Let's Look at an Annotated Cohabitation Agreement," I have set out an entire draft cohabitation agreement and annotated numerous provisions to clarify the goal and purpose of a particular word, paragraph, or clause. As we move through the sections of this chapter, you may want to flip to particular sections of an actual agreement to see what a paragraph may look like and how it might be customized for your needs.

Let's start by considering some very basic matters that can and cannot be put in a cohabitation agreement. You need to concentrate on realistic goals. There is little point in putting in a clause that a court will simply ignore at a later date if a question or problem emerges in the relationship. A cohabitation agreement may contain a couple's agreement on points such as these:

- ownership of property
- use of property
- division of property
- day-to-day operation of the financial and other aspects of the relationship
- support obligations should the relationship change or end
- direction with respect to the education of the children
- direction with respect to the moral training of the children
- any other matter in the settlement of the couple's affairs

A cohabitation agreement may not contain provisions which

- attempt to predetermine custody of or access to children;
- limit the responsibility for child support;
- are considered not to be in the best interests of children;
- attempt to waive financial disclosure;
- prohibit sexual activity with another person should the relationship end, if that prohibition is a precondition to receiving support or property;
- attempt to waive the aforesaid restrictions.

With those basic guidelines in mind, let's look at some of the typical specific needs that can be addressed in a cohabitation agreement.

PROVIDING FOR CHILDREN

While there will be a little overlap in the following discussion, I want to separate for the moment consideration of the couple's own biological children and children from previous relationships. This doesn't mean that the children will be treated differently day-to-day while the relationship is underway; certainly the goal in such families is to truly blend everyone into one happy group. However, the fact remains that blended families face extra challenges because of residential schedules for kids coming and going and financial obligations related to them.

Biological Children of the Couple

Common-law couples have the same concerns about children as legally married couples: they worry about their health, their safety, their education, their moral and religious upbringing, and they have views about such things as how to discipline children, nutrition, not to mention the impact of children on careers. Even issues such as the pursuit of careers in sports or music are serious considerations for some families. All of these issues may be addressed in a cohabitation agreement. Typically couples concentrate on four things:

Education

Will it be public or private?
Will it be a religious school?

Moral/Religious Considerations

Primarily, what will the religious upbringing be, if any?

Discipline

Will there be corporal punishment (and I should say at this time that in my experience this generally means an absolute prohibition on corporal punishment).

Career Changes Dictated by the Arrival of Children

If the children have not yet been born, then little more can be said than setting out wishes, expectations, and intentions with respect to children, if and when they arrive. However, whether the children have actually been born or not, parents often still apply their minds to questions of specific schools, specific religious upbringing and have spelled these out in cohabitation agreements.

It is also important to remember some reality checks such as the availability of sufficient funds to cover private schools. Let's face it, times change and the recent economic troubles saw many families make tough decisions about the affordability of private schools for their children.

This raises another important consideration—the enforceability of such provisions if a common-law partner "changes his or her mind." Will it cause the relationship to end? Will a couple stay together and consider asking a court to force one of them to honour a commitment to a particular religious upbringing?

Consider, for example, Allan and Diane who had agreed to raise their children as Catholics. Diane later became a Jehovah's Witness and wanted the children to be similarly observant. A disagreement of that magnitude usually undermines the entire relationship and court enforcement of the agreement with respect to religious upbringing is pointless in an intact relationship. However, if the couple separates, the court will find their original commitment to a particular faith very, very persuasive and, with that initial agreement in mind, will then make a decision that is in the best interests of the children.

The same is true about commitments to bar the use of corporal punishment. A court will not likely intervene in an intact relationship if the parents have a disagreement about how things are set up, but it will again find the original agreement persuasive in a subsequent custody/access determination should the relationship end. (Tip: courts generally don't support the use of corporal punishment).

The impact of the arrival of children on a career can be profound for both spouses. For example, the mother typically will need to take maternity leave. This may have immediate financial consequences. A father may now have extra financial pressure and responsibilities as the sole breadwinner. He may have an opportunity for paternity leave. How can these changes be addressed?

As we have seen (with very limited exceptions), child support issues cannot be addressed in a cohabitation agreement. Spousal support, however, can be addressed. Let's look at two possible scenarios where the arrival of children, career changes, and spousal support are connected.

A Specific Formula for Childcare When a Career Change Arrives

You will recall from the discussion in Chapter 4, "The Legal Consequences of Living Common Law: Rights and Responsibilities If You Separate," that in the absence of a cohabitation agreement, one spouse's contribution to childcare and household activities can be a reason to justify allocating a portion of the other common-law partner's property to the spouse who provided those services. For example, a common-law couple lives in a property owned entirely by the husband, children are born, career changes are made by the mother (who effectively becomes a stay-at-home mom who runs the lives of the children and the family), and the relationship later ends. That mother may be in a position to argue that it would be unjust for the common-law husband to retain the entire value of that home, given her contribution to childcare and household services.

A way for dealing with this type of issue in a cohabitation agreement can be seen in Chapter 11, "Let's Look at an Annotated Cohabitation Agreement," in particular, the topic of compensation for services. In this approach, the owner of the property in question pays a set amount to the other partner in compensation for the household or childcare services that are provided. This optional approach is designed to address the potentially unjust result of providing the care and then not ending up with a share of any property. You will note that in that particular draft agreement, there is a blanket spousal support release set out in paragraph 3.

Spousal Support, Releases, and Sunset Clauses

In the draft cohabitation agreement provided in Chapter 11, you will find an example of a blanket release of spousal support for a common-law couple. In other words the couple agrees that in the event the relationship ends, either through separation or one partner dying, neither partner has an entitlement to claim spousal support.

As discussed in Chapter 9, "Signed, Sealed, and Delivered," the court reserves the right to ignore spousal support releases if the outcome would be unconscionable for the spouse who is in need. This review of an entitlement to spousal support vis-à-vis the release is usually done in the context of a court examining whether the couple anticipated the circumstances that exist at the time of separation. In other words, when they signed the cohabitation agreement and included the spousal support release, things looked rosy and both spouses appeared to be financially independent, but when they actually separated, or one spouse died, the circumstances were dramatically different.

Let's consider this in the context of children and career changes. If a couple has included a blanket spousal support release but then go on to have children, the arrival of those children has an impact on the career of the mother. For example, because she becomes a stay-at-home mom, she effectively runs the household and the children's lives instead of pursuing her once-promising career, and the couple may end up in a situation that was completely unanticipated at the time they included the blanket spousal support release. How can this be addressed?

Many couples include a clause in the cohabitation agreement that has the effect of nullifying the release in the event of the birth of children. This is sometimes referred to as a "Sunset Provision." If no children are born, there should be no impact on the careers of the couple. If there is no impact on their careers, then they should remain economically self-sufficient and responsible for themselves financially. But if, through a change in plans or if accidents happen, the spousal support release is abandoned and the couple uses a different approach. The different approach could be either to simply state that, in the event of a subsequent separation or death, the laws of the particular province or territory with respect to spousal support will govern.

Alternatively, a formula could be provided setting spousal support at a fixed level. The latter approach can be problematic as it is difficult to anticipate what would be required. My own recommendation is to simply allow the law of the particular province or territory to govern in the event the spousal support release is not going to be relied upon.

Providing for Your Support

This is an important issue for many common-law couples. As we asked in Chapter 4, what happens if you separate and one of you needs financial help? In Chapter 5, we learned that common-law relationships come with the possibility of spousal support obligations. If you separate and one spouse is in financial need and the other spouse has the ability to pay, then spousal support may be ordered. If a spouse dies and the surviving spouse is in financial need again, a claim may be made against the estate for financial support. The approach across Canada has been affected by the arrival of the Spousal Support Advisory Guidelines which provide a formula that divides disposable income between two households depending on the length of the relationship, the age of the parties and other factors. Essentially it still comes down to an assessment of one spouse's need and the other spouse's ability to pay, along with the consideration of the lifestyle to which they have been accustomed. For more detailed information about spousal support, see my book *Surviving Your Divorce, A Guide to Canadian Family Law*, 4th edition, Chapter 7.

What is appropriate for your case? Common-law couples have three options:

- a blanket spousal support release;
- a formula for the calculation of spousal support;
- a statement that they will be covered by provincial law at the time of separation or death of a spouse.

Let's look at each individually.

Blanket Spousal Support Release

With this approach, the couple is saying to each other that, no matter what happens in their lives, neither one of them will be responsible for spousal support to the other. The wording of such a release needs to be comprehensive. See, for example, the topic of Support in Chapter 11. The language contained in that spousal support release clause has been developed by lawyers and judges as an attempt to "bulletproof" the possibility of spouses attempting to obtain spousal support relief once released. Ideally, independent legal advice will have been received at the same time to make it even more invulnerable to attack.

However, there are two challenges with such a release. First, it can be difficult to anticipate the future and who may or may not be in need at the time of a future separation or death of a spouse. Secondly, the courts have reserved the right to disregard such releases if the ultimate circumstances of a spouse are unconscionable. Consider, for example, the possibility of a young couple signing a cohabitation agreement which contains a spousal support release. Many years later, after the arrival of children, and perhaps financial setbacks for the family, a breakdown in the relationship occurs and the wife, faced with a spousal support release, must apply for welfare. The court would have a difficult time enforcing a spousal support release in such circumstances, as clearly the wife's situation had not been anticipated by the couple many years previously.

However, barring truly unfair circumstances, and in particular in the presence of effective independent legal advice, the court will enforce the release.

For example, in the case of one Canadian couple, their marriage contract was signed five years into a stormy marriage that had involved numerous separations, the couple finally separated twelve years after they signed a marriage contract. That agreement had been drafted by the husband's lawyer and had gone through a number of redrafts that included the wife receiving independent legal advice. At the time the matter finally arrived before a judge, the wife was close to bankruptcy in part because she had been obsessively litigating the case and incurring legal fees. Even though she clearly had a financial need, the court did not consider those circumstances to be unconscionable and enforced the marriage contract against her. The same would be true with respect to a cohabitation agreement.

When considering what the court might ultimately think of your agreement and whether it includes a spousal support release, keep in mind the words of the Supreme Court of Canada, which stated in a 2009 case that "the best way to protect the finality of any negotiated agreement in family law, is to ensure both its procedural and substantive integrity in accordance with the relevant legislative scheme." In other words, be fair in the way that you negotiate and be fair in terms of the content of your cohabitation agreement.

Develop Your Own Special Formula

As an alternative to a blanket spousal support release that may be subject to challenge at a later date, some common-law couples develop and use their own spousal support calculation formula. This formula can be related to the respective incomes of the couple; it can be developed on the basis of potential need, or it can simply be the selection of an arbitrary but reasonable figure. For example, consider the case of Craig and Valerie. At the time they began their cohabitation, Craig earned a salary that was consistently in the $300,000 per annum range. Valerie, on the other hand, earned an income of approximately $60,000 to $70,000 per annum. If they separated, or if Craig died and they did not have a cohabitation agreement dictating some approach to spousal support, then clearly Valerie would likely have a claim for spousal support against Craig or his estate. In their cohabitation agreement, Craig and Valerie acknowledged the differential in their income and stated instead that in the event of separation or Craig's death, and if the relationship lasted more than five years, Craig's obligation for spousal support to Valerie would be to a maximum of $70,000. In other words, if the consequence of the relationship to Valerie was to suffer an income less than $70,000, Craig would make up the difference. If Valerie was earning at least $70,000 at the time of separation, there would be no support.

In addition, when developing such formulas, couples will need to consider the length of the relationship. It is possible, for example, to tie the length of any possible support obligation to the length of the relationship. In other words, if the relationship is two years in length, spousal support, if ordered, will not exceed two years. If the relationship is ten years in length, spousal support would not exceed a set period. If these formulas are negotiated in good faith and are reasonable and in particular if there has been effective independent legal advice, the court will enforce them.

Agree to Be Governed by Provincial Law at the Point of Separation

In some cases, a common-law couple has developed and signed the cohabitation agreement more out of concern for property issues than spousal support. Rather than try to develop a formula or predict the future, or to hope that a spousal support release will be enforced, the couple agrees to simply be bound by the provincial law of a particular jurisdiction as of the date of separation or death of a spouse. At that point, the couple would ask to have their spousal support obligations calculated in accordance with the law and would agree to be bound by the court's decision in that eventuality.

In this regard, see the upcoming section Dispute Resolution, in which we consider some alternatives to going to court. It may be possible, for example, to participate in a mediation or arbitration through which a reasonable spousal support figure is calculated at the time of separation or the time of death of a spouse. This approach may be advisable in the situation where a common-law spouse has entered the relationship and by doing so has lost the entitlement to spousal support from a previous spouse.

Providing for Death, Injury, or Illness

As we have seen in Chapter 5, common-law couples face even greater challenges than legally married couples face when confronted with these types of problems. Rights or responsibilities may or may not flow for a common-law spouse depending on the jurisdiction in which you reside. See, for example, the Table of Common Law Rights and Responsibilities set out in Appendix D. Let's consider these challenges in two separate categories: (1) illness and injury and (2) death.

Illness and Injury

At a minimum, each common-law spouse must have a Power of Attorney for Personal Care and a Power of Attorney for Property (note that in some provinces these documents have different legal names, such as a "mandate," but the legal affect is the same). Powers of attorney allow an appointed individual to make decisions when the grantor of the power of attorney is unable to make those decisions on his or her own behalf. In the case of a Power of Attorney for Personal Care, these decisions may relate to treatment in hospital or extended care.

In the case of a Power of Attorney for Property, it allows an appointed individual to make bank deposits, pay bills, and even operate a business on behalf of a person incapable of doing so as a result of injury or illness. I cannot stress enough the importance in today's society of having these documents in place. Medical science has been able to work wonders to keep individuals alive after even the most catastrophic injury. No one hopes or expects to be in such a position, but the granting of authority to deal with your care and property should this happen can be invaluable. Whether you choose to grant this authority to your common-law spouse is a separate question. In some cases, a couple may grant the authority for personal care to their spouse, but the Power of Attorney for Property to a separate individual who has perhaps more experience in dealing with financial issues. Regardless, the individuals who have been given this authority must work cooperatively to ensure first and foremost that your care is provided. The power of attorney is as important as a will and if all planning has gone well, at the end of this exercise, you should have not only a cohabitation agreement but also wills and powers of attorney which work together.

Wills

As we have seen in Chapter 5, a will is of critical importance. If one is not in place, a deceased person is considered to have died intestate and it is necessary for the court to appoint an individual to manage the estate of the deceased individual. This adds not only to the cost and delay surrounding the deceased's property, but also to the confusion and distress of his or her family members. You are doing your survivors a great favour by planning ahead through the use of a will.

Statutory entitlements to a share of property upon the death of a common-law spouse vary from province to province across Canada. Again, see the schedules set out in Appendix D, "Rights and Responsibilities of Common-Law Couples." Common-law couples cannot take for granted their ability to receive a reasonable share of property in the event of the death of a spouse. They, more than married couples, must specifically contemplate what will happen to their property in the event of the death of a spouse.

In the draft cohabitation agreement provided in Chapter 11, paragraph 13(f) states that neither common-law spouse will claim any interest in the estate of the other except as specifically provided for in a will that has been made by the deceased spouse, or, in the case of intestacy, as may be provided by the laws of the particular province or territory which governs the death of the common-law spouse. In most provinces, a surviving common-law spouse will have no property claim on the estate of a deceased partner as the laws governing estates do not provide surviving common-law couples with property rights. In the case of legal marriages, surviving spouses have automatic legal rights to claim a share of an intestate estate. This has meant that it is even more important for common-law couples to apply their minds to what happens in the event of the death of a common-law spouse. As stated above, paragraph 13(f) states that a surviving common-law spouse will receive only what is provided in a will. This will may or may not be shared with the common-law spouse. In a trusting relationship, common-law spouses do joint estate planning. In the absence of a will, or in the case of a will that leaves nothing to a surviving common-law spouse, paragraph 13(m) requires the heirs, executors, and administrators of a deceased common-law spouse to be bound by the cohabitation agreement and to do all things necessary to carry out the terms of the agreement as may be applicable at the time of the common-law spouse's death.

The net effect of a validly made cohabitation agreement is that it may operate and have the same effect as a will. Consider the situation in which Warren and Bonnie have resided in a common-law relationship for 20 years. They signed a cohabitation agreement in which Warren set out extensive categories of independent property, as did Bonnie. Warren, however, did not make a will, despite Bonnie's repeated efforts to have him do so. When Warren passed away suddenly, Bonnie needed to know the consequences of his death for the property which they used during their cohabitation. An administrator for the estate of Warren would be appointed and that administrator would look to the cohabitation agreement to see what it provided in terms of Warren's property. The administrator would see that Warren had an extensive category of independent property to which Bonnie had no entitlement. The administrator would look to determine who, under the applicable provincial or territorial law, would be entitled to inherit Warren's property.

If Warren had children from a previous relationship, they would very likely stand first in line to inherit all of Warren's assets as defined as independent property in the cohabitation agreement. In addition, property that Warren held jointly with Bonnie would need to be reconciled and its value divided between Warren's beneficiaries and Bonnie. Perhaps this is what Warren intended. However, if it is not what he intended, Bonnie may certainly be left in an awkward position *vis-à-vis* Warren's children from a previous relationship. It would have likely been much less expensive and less confusing if Warren had simply made a will stating that, while certain property would be treated as independent in the event of separation, it might be treated as joint property in the event of death.

For example, if Warren and Bonnie occupied a home, Warren may have wished that that home would be treated as independent property if he and Bonnie separated, but Bonnie's sole property if Warren should pass away. These types of consequences need to be contemplated at the time the cohabitation agreement is negotiated and drafted. It may also mean, depending on the length of the relationship and other events such as the arrival of children, that the cohabitation agreement will need a revision and updating as the relationship evolves.

Consider, for example, the usefulness of triggering events that change the impact of the agreement on property depending on the circumstances of the relationship. Warren could exclude a home in a category of independent property unless and until the relationship lasts a certain period of time or children are born. If either of those triggering events occurs, Warren and Bonnie's cohabitation agreement could include a provision that the home moves from the category of independent property to the category of shared property and, particularly in the event of his death, becomes the sole property of Bonnie.

You will recall my statement at the outset of this book that a cohabitation agreement should be seen in the context of estate planning. Cohabitation agreements, powers of attorney, and wills should all work in conjunction.

What About Your Property?

This is probably the most common reason for a common-law couple to need or consider a cohabitation agreement. One or both of them are concerned about the impact of cohabitation on their property. It can be property that they already own and wish to protect, or it may be property that they will be acquiring in the future and wish to protect.

As we can see in Appendix D, the treatment of property for common-law couples varies from province to province. In most provinces, common-law couples acquire no statutory right to claim an interest in property and must sue to establish an entitlement if they invested money or labour in property in the name of the other spouse. This is an essential concern for common-law couples—the lack of statutory property rights. In fact, the entire reason many people live in a common-law relationship rather than a legal marriage is to avoid the consequences of the property-sharing schemes contained in provincial law. The differences in approaches from province to province, the differences in needs between common-law couples, particularly for those who are entering common-law relationships after a previous relationship that perhaps ended through divorce or death, make it imperative for common-law couples to think carefully about the impact of the relationship on their property.

A number of the options available to couples are as follows:

- They may shield particular categories of property from division at any time in the future.
- They may create a special scheme for division of their property.
- They may use a combination of a special scheme and sunset provisions.

Let's consider each one.

Shield Particular Categories of Property

In this approach, the couple applies their minds to the property which they will bring into the relationship and property that they may acquire while the relationship is underway. Consider, for example, the approach taken in the draft agreement provided in Chapter 11. See paragraph 3, Classes of Property to Remain Separate. In this approach, the parties define what will be considered independent property: that is, property that will remain the sole and exclusive property of the individual who owns it. The agreement acknowledges their ownership at the outset of the relationship and that their ownership shall continue unimpeded throughout the relationship and in the event that the relationship should end through ceasing cohabitation or the death of a spouse.

Paragraph 4 of the draft agreement goes on to provide a list of categories which shall be considered independent property and, therefore, not divided. This includes, for example, the property that is set out in Schedules A and B attached to the cohabitation agreement (see Appendices A and B). In the draft agreement, it also provides that any property acquired by a common-law spouse after the date of cohabitation, but in that spouse's name alone, shall not be divided and will be treated as independent property.

Paragraph 4, as included in the draft agreement, is comprehensive and sets out, for example, the possibility of excluding all income, all gifts, all property received as damages and all property that is inherited. In this approach, the common-law couples apply their minds specifically to categories of property and specifically exclude them from any possibility of sharing.

A consideration that will arise in using this approach is what happens to property that is converted during the course of cohabitation? In other words, what if a piece of independent property such as a houseboat is sold and the proceeds from the sale are then invested in a motorcycle? Is the newly acquired property also treated as independent property?

Examine paragraph 10 in the draft agreement provided in Chapter 11. In this paragraph, the parties agree that, if it becomes necessary to divide their property and either party has converted a piece of independent property, then a guide to division of the newly acquired property is set out. In this approach, which is simply an example of dealing with such property, the parties deduct the value of the initial piece of independent property from the value of the newly acquired piece of property and then divide the net equity remaining after such a credit is given to the person who originally owned the piece of independent property. For example, using the houseboat and motorcycle example, if the houseboat was sold for $25,000 and the owner of the houseboat used the proceeds to acquire a motorcycle that, at the time of separation, was valued at $50,000, the owner of the independent property would receive a credit of $25,000 for his or her initial investment and then the parties would divide equally the remaining equity of $25,000, thereby each receiving $12,500.

As I stated earlier, this is simply one approach to dealing with the tracing of the value of independent property into subsequently acquired assets. An alternative approach is to simply exclude the entire value of any subsequently acquired assets. Again, using the example of the houseboat and the motorcycle, the couple could agree that any property acquired with the proceeds of sale of a piece of independent property is entirely excluded. In other words, the $25,000 used from the houseboat to acquire a motorcycle that is ultimately worth $50,000 would result in the entire exclusion of the value of the motorcycle. It is up to the couple to decide which type of approach they would prefer to use.

Create a Special Scheme for Division of Property

Here, the couple states simply that they have developed their own method of dividing property in the event of separation or death. Options include:

1. **A separate property scheme** by which each spouse agrees that they will keep whatever he or she acquired in his or her own name. In other words, if something is registered in one spouse's name, he or she keeps that property. If a piece of property is not registered in any particular spouse's name, for example, furniture, then whoever paid for the asset keeps that asset. This is an approach that keeps the parties entirely separate as to the acquisition and ownership of property. In the event a piece of property is acquired jointly, the presumption is that the property is divided equally between them.
2. **A community property scheme**. This approach is probably best considered as the opposite of the separate property scheme because, in this approach, all property regardless of the way in which it is owned, registered or in which title is held, or how it is paid for, is simply divided equally. In effect, the common-law couple agrees to treat their property as if they were married. Why would a couple do so? You will recall from Chapter 1, that some couples are required to live common law because they are unable to marry. They may be unable to complete their divorce from a previous spouse, or they consider the common-law relationship to be the equivalent of a marriage and simply agree in their cohabitation agreement to be treated as if they were married. If such a provision is included in a cohabitation agreement, the couple need only state that, in the event of separation or divorce, their property will

be governed in accordance with the *Family Law* property rules for their province, the date of marriage will be considered to be the date of their cohabitation as reflected in the agreement, and their date of separation will be as defined by provincial family law.

3. **An alternative for division of property** is to create categories of property, not unlike the statutory schemes that were provided many years ago in some provinces. For example, in Ontario, prior to the *Family Law Act*, 1986, Ontario couples divided their property into two pools, family assets, and non-family assets. "Family assets" were defined as including such things as the home in which the parties resided, family savings, family furniture, family vehicles, family cottage, and other types of property used by the husband and wife and/or the children. Separate from family assets was a category of non-family assets. This was defined to include businesses, pensions, personal investments, and any other category of property that was specifically identified. In this approach, the couple states that family assets will be divided equally between the couple in the event of separation or the death of a spouse, while non-family assets (which are really the equivalent of the independent property discussed earlier) will not be divided. In using such an approach, though, a couple must be careful to continuously monitor their use of assets. What becomes of a business that, at the time of the agreement, was operated from a traditional office tower downtown but has subsequently moved into a home office in whose operation the other spouse becomes involved? Will that be a non-family or family asset? It is certainly not impossible to use such a family asset scheme and it may work very well for many common-law couples, but it does mean that the parties must be alert.
4. **The couple uses a combination of approaches.** In the upcoming section, Sunset Provisions and Termination Clauses, we will consider the use of a provision that triggers a different approach. Depending on an event in the context of property division, a couple may agree that one approach to property division will be used unless and until a particular event occurs. Consider, for example, the possibility of a couple agreeing that they shall be separate as to property unless and until children are born, at which time their

> approach to property division shall convert to one of a community of property. In other words, the couple may agree to use two different approaches depending on how the relationship evolves.

The draft agreement set out in Chapter 11, uses an approach that combines the exclusion of independent property and the sharing of jointly acquired property. I included this particular draft as it works well for the majority of common-law couples who seek to protect categories of property, but who also wish to share property that they acquire jointly throughout the relationship. The draft agreement also protects against the possibility of spouses unexpectedly acquiring interests in property because of financial investment, labour, household services, or child care duties. See, for example, paragraph 5 which expressly prohibits the acquisition of an interest in a category of independent property because of a variety of circumstances that may occur during the relationship.

Special comment is needed with respect to gifts. You will note, in paragraph 6 of the draft agreement provided in Chapter 11, that these various approaches to division of property by common-law couples do not need to inhibit the ability of spouses to make gifts or transfers to each other. For example, one spouse wishes to make a gift of the houseboat or motorcycle to the other spouse possible. In other words, the imposition of categories of independent property does not prevent the transfer of a property in that category between the spouses. However, as you will see in paragraph 7 of the draft agreement, to avoid confusion it may be best to cap the value of gifts that do not need to be tracked in writing. Paragraph 7 provides that property of less than $1,000 in value can be given without any written evidence. However, once property that has a value over $1,000 is transferred or gifted to the other spouse, it must be evidenced in writing. This again is to avoid confusion at a later date.

A special comment is required with respect to homes used by common-law couples. Typically a home owned prior to cohabitation will be shielded from division through the use of a cohabitation agreement. In other words, if a common-law spouse retained a home from a previous divorce through their own work and savings prior to cohabiting, they are often particularly concerned about the possibility of being required to share the value of that property at a later date if the common-law relationship is not successful or if one spouse dies. As we have seen in the previous paragraphs, it is possible to shield that property as a category known as independent property.

Paragraph 13 of the draft cohabitation agreement provides some guidance with respect to household and personal expenses. Note, however, subparagraph (e) dealing with the home. It confirms again that the ownership of the home is independent property, and then goes on to explain how expenses related to that home will be divided. Importantly, subparagraph 13(e)(iii) deals with a notice to the spouse who does not have an interest in that property to vacate the property.

Let's consider, for example, the situation of a common-law couple, William and Libby. William brought a home into the common-law relationship and excluded it from division by characterizing it as independent property in their cohabitation agreement. Unfortunately, after five years of cohabitation, Libby and William have had difficult times in their relationship and will be separating. Libby, however, is comfortable and does not wish to leave William's home unless and until she finds suitable accommodations. How long must William wait before Libby vacates his home? He is becoming concerned because of the increasing acrimony between them; he has learned that Libby is now seeing another person, and feels awkward when Libby brings that individual into his home. This type of awkward situation is avoided by a paragraph that allows William to give Libby "Notice to Vacate." It also goes on to provide in subparagraph (iv) that, during the period of notice, Libby will not entertain anyone in the home, nor will she make any alterations to it. It also provides an extra level of protection for William should the relationship break down and the estate trustee or executor of William's estate need to obtain vacant possession of William's home in the event that William passes away.

As this can be one of the most important components of a cohabitation agreement, take your time in developing the worksheets and schedules of property as set out in the appendices. Work with your partner to agree in principle on the types of property that will be excluded and the types of property that will be shared. With an open and fair approach, it should be possible to reach an agreement that suits both your interests.

Sunset Provisions and Termination Clauses

It is possible to include provisions in your cohabitation agreement that will bring it or specific provisions in it to an end upon the occurrence of a particular event. For example, Teri and Bruce are going to be living common law but both of them are uncertain about the relationship.

They want to see how a number of things unfold:

- Will they both remain in Vancouver, or will one of them be transferred to another province or country?
- Will they be able to live together after each has lived on their own and been independent for many years?
- Will they have children?

Even with all these questions they are willing to give it a try.

To deal with some of these concerns, they decide to include a spousal support release in their cohabitation agreement. However, they also agree that if a child is born and one or both of them is required or chooses to take time out from their career to care for the child, then the spousal support release will not apply. This would mean that if they later separated, either of them could ask for spousal support to be ordered under the applicable provincial law at that time, or they could decide to include in their cohabitation agreement a set formula for the calculation of spousal support at that time.

Similarly, consider Debbi and Mike who are living common law in a home that was owned by Mike before they began to cohabit. They have agreed in their cohabitation agreement that the home will not be shared in the event of a separation. However, they also include a Sunset Provision that provides for Mike's house to be shared equally in the event the relationship lasts more than 15 years or if a child is born and they reside in the home as a family.

The beauty of a cohabitation agreement is the ability to include flexible provisions which can protect the couple's interests but also allow for a different approach later in their relationship.

Managing the Household Budgets and Other Matters

Most of the discussion in this chapter has focused on management of issues that arise upon separation or the death of a spouse. These are not the only challenges or areas that cohabitation agreements can deal with. Many couples need to consider the operation of their household budget and other matters and choose to use a cohabitation agreement as a way of managing those issues.

Financial concerns are often at the forefront. See, for example, paragraph 13 of the draft cohabitation agreement in Chapter 11, which sets out an approach to dealing with household and personal expenses. These provisions are simply examples. In subparagraph (a), the parties have agreed that they will share equally all costs relating to food, household goods, furniture and appliance repair. An alternative could be for the parties to acknowledge their different earning powers and divide these expenses instead in proportion to their annual incomes to achieve a more equitable allocation. Alternatively again, the couple could divide specific categories of expenses so that, for example, the common-law husband handles the mortgage, realty taxes and utilities, while the common-law wife handles food, household requirements, furniture acquisitions and the like. There are no limits on the variations that can be used in handling these kinds of expenses.

Similarly, consider subparagraph 13 (b) which invites the parties to discuss how they will manage their banking for expenses. In this case, the parties have agreed that they will face their respective contributions for family expenses into a joint bank account. An alternative would be for the couple to agree to maintain entirely separate bank account management.

In subparagraph 13 (c) of the draft agreement, the parties have agreed that they will each pay for all other living expenses such as their clothing, holidays, medical, dental, and even prescription drug expenses. Similar provisions are set out with respect to children and in the event that there are children from a previous relationship. It is possible for common-law couples to agree even on the allocation of child support payments that are received to various expenses related to those children. You will recall the discussion in Chapter 3 concerning rights and responsibilities while living together without a cohabitation agreement, and in particular the various situations in which many find themselves when they are blending children and when child support and/or spousal support payments are being received from other households. It is my recommendation that these payments or obligations be acknowledged in the cohabitation agreement so that there is no confusion over who is paying for what, particularly as it relates to children.

What other types of things governing a day-to-day lifestyle may couples need to provide for in cohabitation agreements? Again, the sky is the limit, but consider the following possibilities:

- vacations
- sporting activities
- participation in clubs and other memberships
- acknowledgment of commitments to pay for elderly parents
- completion of education
- acknowledgment of career aspirations and support thereof
- acknowledgment of religious preferences and tolerance thereof
- acknowledgment of special needs children
- acknowledgment of medical issues and special needs for one of the spouses

The list is long and the only caution that I add in terms including provisions that attempt to govern the day-to-day operation of the relationship is the ability to enforce the agreement. There is little point in including a provision that someone will take out the garbage or mow the lawn if enforcement of it is virtually impossible. Instead, I would recommend focusing on matters of genuine importance to the relationship itself.

What if We Get Married after Signing a Cohabitation Agreement?

As we saw in Chapter 1, one of the typical reasons for a couple to live common law is "I want to give the relationship a trial run before deciding on marriage."

We hope that a solid cohabitation agreement has contributed to the development of a solid relationship, so the last thing that we want to see is that the cohabitation agreement inhibits the relationship evolving into a solid marriage. If the parties worry that taking a step towards marriage would unravel their contract, then the contract is not contributing to a strengthening of the relationship; it is hurting it. No one would relish the idea of having to renegotiate the contract simply to get married.

Provincial and territorial family law provides that if the parties to a cohabitation agreement marry each other, the agreement is deemed to be a marriage contract. The terms of the agreement continue as written subject to any terms that come into effect in the event of marriage. As we saw in the section Sunset and Termination Provisions, it is possible to include a term that triggers an end to the contract itself or certain provisions in it. Such a triggering event could be the marriage of the parties.

However, in the absence of such a provision, the contract will automatically become a marriage contract and be enforced as such. It will also be subject to all of the same potential challenges to its validity as reviewed in Chapter 9.

Conditional Gifts from Third Parties

Some spouses receive gifts from their parents or family members. Perhaps a parent has given the couple a home to live in, but they have also included a condition that the property cannot be sold or mortgaged unless the parents consent. To protect their conditional gift they ask the common-law spouses to sign a cohabitation agreement acknowledging the arrangement. If this is desirable for the couple, they still need to be aware that the parents (or what is known as the "donors of the gift") are automatically considered to be parties to the contract for the purpose of enforcement or amendment of the contract. So, accept such conditional gifts as a part of a cohabitation agreement, but recognize that you have contractual partners—the in-laws.

Contracts Made Outside Ontario

A cohabitation agreement made in another province or territory, or even another country, can be enforced in other provinces or territories of Canada provided it meets the proper law for contracts generally and meets the standards of our law for cohabitation agreements. Support provisions can still be overturned by the courts if unfair. Custody and access agreements will not be enforced if they are deemed to be not in the best interests of the children.

If anyone is thinking that they can simply go out of Canada and create a cohabitation agreement that is valid in the country in which it is signed but not in compliance with Canadian law, they should not expect that agreement to be enforced here. Our courts will not let a foreign cohabitation agreement do an end run on our rules.

Minors and the Mentally Incapable

Surprisingly, minors can sign cohabitation agreements but the agreement will be subject to the approval of the court. That approval can be obtained before or after the cohabitation agreement is signed. Mentally incapable people may also enter into cohabitation agreements, but their legal guardians will need to approve or sign the contract on their behalf.

Breakup to Makeup: Reconciliation

Cohabitation agreements may be made under unusual circumstances. Consider, for example, the situation of Rick and Jan, who have been cohabiting off and on for several years. The relationship has had some serious ups and downs, mostly related to uneven work opportunities for both of them. However, they don't want to stop trying to make the relationship work. A cohabitation agreement has been proposed by Rick to deal with the question of their assets and spousal support. Neither one of them wants to be paying support to the other if things don't work out. In drafting the agreement, they confront a key issue: What happens to the agreement if they do what they always seem to do every couple of years—break up and then get back together?

The releases contained in the cohabitation agreement and, in particular, the spousal support release, will operate if they separate. If they later reconcile, do the contract's terms need to be refreshed or do they still apply if they break up again? What if real estate transactions have occurred after the separation, but before they reconcile? Will those transactions stand? Unfortunately, there are no clear answers on questions such as this and it is therefore advisable to deal specifically with the possibility in the agreement by stating that the contract applies to the relationship unless the agreement is revoked or amended and that its terms will not lose any force or effect should they separate and then reconcile and then separate again.

In one case, Mr. and Ms. Ogilvy had separated and they consulted their lawyers. After receiving some advice, Ms. Ogilvy didn't like the way in which the law would treat her and decided to reconcile with her husband and then wait for a "better time." The court looked at the situation and decided that her decision was "a reconciliation of convenience" and not genuine. The earlier date of separation continued to apply.

Enforcement of the Cohabitation Agreement

We, of course, hope that once the agreement is negotiated and signed, it can simply be filed away with your wills and powers of attorney and forgotten while you lead a happy common-law life. However, there may come a day when it must be pulled out, dusted off and considered in the context of a separation, illness, injury, or death of a partner. How is the contract then used? Let's look at two possibilities.

Property Issues

Once a couple separates or one of the couple dies and the issue of division of property emerges, the cohabitation agreement is supposed to be used to help clarify the situation. The Schedules A and B that were so meticulously crafted are reviewed to clarify which property was owned when the relationship began and which property is to be treated as independent property and not shared. Title to those assets should be clear. The agreement should also provide guidance for the division of property that was acquired during the period of cohabitation. However, if a claim is made against an asset of the other spouse, the cohabitation agreement is raised as a defence to the claim.

As you will see in Chapter 11, the terms of the contract are also binding on the heirs, executors, estate trustees, and administrators of a deceased common-law spouse. This means that if the surviving common-law spouse attempts to make a claim against property that was not intended to be shared, the estate's trustee is obliged to enforce the cohabitation agreement to preserve the assets for the correct beneficiaries of the deceased common-law spouse.

Enforcement of an entitlement to support or a release of support.

If the cohabitation agreement contains a blanket release of any entitlement to claim support, it will be used in the same way as the cohabitation agreement was used to protect independent property from claims by a common-law spouse. In other words, the common-law spouse may apply to the court for spousal support, the spouse against whom the claim is made simply files the cohabitation agreement in defence of that claim. If the spouse making the claim cannot convince a court that the spousal support release should be thrown out, then the court will have no choice but to dismiss the claim for spousal support.

Alternatively, the cohabitation agreement may contain a provision that comes into force upon separation or death. You will recall from the above section Providing for Your Support that a possible scenario (an alternative to a complete release of spousal support) is to actually provide a fixed amount that will be paid for a fixed period of time to transition a separating common-law spouse (if she or he is in need) to a new independent life. Consider, for example, a provision such as this: "In the event of the parties cohabiting less than forty-eight months and then separating, the husband will pay the wife the sum of $5,000 per month for a period of twelve months, at which time the entitlement to spousal support shall terminate absolutely and be released. No variation of this provision is possible."

If the husband then refused to pay the support that he had agreed to pay, how can the agreement be enforced? Most provinces contain a provision similar to Ontario's Section 35 of the *Family Law Act*, which provides that the cohabitation agreement may be filed with the court. Once filed, a clause related to support may be enforced as if it was an Order of the Court. This type of enforcement need not be included in the contract itself as it is available by law, but it would be advisable to check with your local lawyer to confirm that a similar provision is available. To be absolutely certain, it may be advisable to include in the cohabitation agreement a provision stating that any agreement with respect to spousal support may be enforced by filing the agreement with the court.

Dispute Resolution

There are a variety of methods available to resolve disputes in family law matters. Traditionally, the primary method has been to go to court to litigate in an adversarial environment. Each side is pitted against the other, trying to poke holes in each other's case and trying to convince a judge that their "version of the truth" is the correct one. The court process can be slow, emotionally tough, and financially draining. Lawyers are paid by the hour and the justice system is slow. That is a bad combination when it comes to your wallet.

Due to the pain and expense of the court process and the lack of flexibility available to judges (they can only issue a limited number of court orders), alternatives to court have emerged —mediation, arbitration, and collaborative law. Let's look at each briefly.

Mediation

In mediation, a couple facing a family problem such as the interpretation of a provision in a cohabitation agreement may use a skilled third party to assist them in discussing the issue, to reach a mutually satisfactory solution. Instead of having a judge impose a solution, the couple involved designs their own. There is no limit on the type of issue suited to mediation. Its approach is different from the adversarial courtroom, because the mediator encourages the couple to look at the problem from different angles and to develop an understanding of each person's needs and interests The goal is not to develop two competing positions, but to determine whether everyone's interests can be met through some creative solution. After all, who is better able to develop such a solution? A judge who is a complete stranger, or the parties to the dispute themselves?

Mediation is voluntary and non-adversarial. It works best when using a skilled, impartial mediator to guide the discussion. Those who have used mediation have commented that it provided them with new negotiation skills that then permitted them to resolve subsequent disagreements on their own. In a nutshell, mediation seems to be faster and less expensive, and it makes people happier with the agreement. This in turn leads to an increased likelihood that the couple will comply with the agreement that was reached. Provincial and Territorial laws as well as the *Divorce Act* encourage couples to use mediation to solve problems, particularly those related to children.

Does the use of a mediator exclude the need for a lawyer? In a word, no. The mediator helps a couple work on a solution that is mutually agreeable. It is still advisable to take that solution to a lawyer for an opinion as to whether it is in compliance with the law and in each person's best interests. The mediator will often ask whether the mediation should be "open" or "closed." If the mediation is "open," then statements made in mediation may be admissible later in court. If it is "closed," it is the opposite. Everything said in the discussions is confidential and cannot be repeated later.

At the conclusion of mediation, the mediator will prepare what's known as a "memorandum of understanding." This memorandum can be taken to the lawyers for an opinion on whether it is in compliance with the law and whether it meets everyone's interests. If it does, then it can be incorporated into an agreement that is signed and the parties are governed by a new contract. Some couples use mediation to negotiate and design the actual cohabitation agreement from the outset.

Arbitration

In an arbitration process, the parties select a private individual, often an experienced lawyer or a retired judge to hear their dispute in private. It is essentially a private court with a private judge and is attractive for a variety of reasons. First of all, it is completely private. The public and the press (if that is a concern) do not have access to your private affairs. It can be significantly faster and more predictable than the public courts which are busy and subject to delays. One of the primary attractions of arbitration in family law is the ability to select an arbitrator who is an expert in the field. In the justice system, judges are regularly rotated and there is no guarantee that the judge who hears your case will be an expert or interested in a family law matter. The arbitration process will go much more quickly if an expert arbitrator has been hired.

The expense of arbitration can be a weakness. The parties are paying usually for two lawyers, now they are paying for a private judge as well. True, the cost of the arbitrator is being shared by both parties, but it is an additional expense. The only offsetting saving is that if the process goes more quickly, there may actually be net savings.

There are restrictions in provincial law about the use of arbitration in family law cases. It is now becoming a common requirement for couples to obtain independent legal advice prior to entering into a private judicial process.

Collaborative Family Law

There's been a great deal of discussion about a new approach to solving family law problems. It is called "collaborative law" and bears a strong resemblance to mediation. Collaborative law is a blend of soft advocacy on behalf of the couple and the use of well-known mediation techniques. The parties do not use a mediator, but rather they and their lawyers enter into an agreement committing each individual to reach a negotiated settlement that is creative and allows each to think outside the box of traditional family law. The clients and the lawyers expressly forego any entitlement to take the matter to court while the negotiations are underway. This means that the threat of stopping the negotiations and going to court over a particular issue is removed. The lawyers promise to the clients that if the negotiation is unsuccessful, and the matter does have to go to court, then the parties will not use those lawyers and will be forced to retain new lawyers. The intention is to keep the people at the table negotiating, rather than dashing off to court. Collaborative law is still in its early days and it is not for everyone, but it is certainly an attractive alternative for couples who are able to work collaboratively and in good faith.

These methods of resolving problems are relevant to common law couples who are negotiating a cohabitation agreement because it is useful at the outset to contemplate how any disputes will be resolved, should they arise at a later date. For this reason, I recommend including a dispute resolution clause in the cohabitation agreement that states that the parties, when confronted with any dispute related to the agreement, will do as follows:

- attempt to negotiate directly a solution
- negotiate, perhaps with the assistance of lawyers, to obtain a solution
- use mediation and/or arbitration if appropriate, and only use the courts to litigate as a last resort (providing a method of ensuring a calm and, I hope, inexpensive approach to solving problems that may arise from time to time)

In this chapter, which I hope you have read in conjunction with Chapter 11, I have set out many of the typical issues confronted by common-law couples and demonstrated how a cohabitation agreement may be used to address those issues. The list in this chapter is not intended to be exhaustive; every couple has its unique challenge, problem, or need. Anything is possible within the parameters set out in this "Overview of a Cohabitation Agreement." As long as a provision does not affect custody of or access to children, limit child support, is not contrary to the best interests of a child, attempts to waive disclosure, or violates some of the other restrictions, and can be reasonably enforceable, then it can be included in a cohabitation agreement. Just remember: be fair, be open, and use the contract to meet your needs and the needs of your children.

In the next chapter we're going to look at a non-legal challenge in framing a cohabitation agreement: "How to have the conversation with your partner in a way that does not get you off on the wrong foot."

7

HAVING "THE CONVERSATION"

A conversation about the need to have a cohabitation agreement can be awkward. That's especially true if you haven't planned to have the discussion with your partner, if you have no purpose or goal in mind for the discussion, if you cannot articulate the reason for the agreement, if you have no time to work through the contents of the agreement, or if you have sprung the idea of cohabitation agreement on your partner at the last minute.

On the other hand, if you have a plan, an understanding of why this agreement can benfit the relationship, a purpose that you can articulate, enough time to work on the details, access to legal advice if needed, and if you are prepared to work together, then the conversation can be a relationship strengthener all by itself.

Let's consider some of the time things to do and some of the things to avoid when getting ready to have this conversation.

THE "DO'S"

The following are six positive steps that you can take to ensure a productive discussion.

Do have a purpose and make a plan.

Just by reading this book, you are well on your way to having a plan for what can and can't be in a cohabitation agreement. Now you need to start putting details that are personal to the two of you into the plan. Take a quick look at My Cohabitation Agreement Worksheet in the appendices. It will help you get organized and assist you in preparing your plan. In particular, complete the schedule of assets and liabilities. This will ultimately be attached to your cohabitation agreement, and both of you will need to prepare these summary sheets in as much detail as possible.

Gather the documents that support the items referred to in your schedule of assets and liabilities. If you have a student loan, get the paperwork showing the balance owing; if you own a home with a mortgage on it, get the entire file related to your purchase and financing. The lawyer who handled the transaction will have copies of the title documents and mortgage along with any other details. If, for example, your parents loaned or gave you some money for a down payment, this may be shown on the lawyer summary called a Statement of Adjustments. These types of documents are important to show when an asset was acquired, how much it cost, and where the funds came from when the asset was purchased.

As you will see in Chapter 9, "Signed, Sealed, and Delivered," financial disclosure is a very, very important part of preparing an enforceable cohabitation agreement. It is now critical to the validity of these contracts that all assets and liabilities be disclosed as well as their actual values. For example, disclosing that you own a home is not enough, you need its current value and the amount owing on the mortgage.

Do have an answer to the question "Why do we need a cohabitation agreement?"

Think of the moment when you broach the subject with your partner. Imagine he or she turning to you with a surprised look and asking, "Why do we need a cohabitation agreement?" How prepared are you for this? Is it because you are concerned about your financial picture? Is one of you carrying a debt load? Is it because you're worried about what will happen to property you own once you begin cohabitation? Is it because you are blending a family and children?

Keep in mind that your partner may be completely unaware of the possibility of a contract helping your relationship. So it's imperative, when questions arise, to have a clear answer such as: "Well, I have done a little research, and because we will be living in [or are already living in] my home, which is all I have managed to hang onto from my divorce, we need to be clear about ownership, how we will manage our budget, things like realty taxes, how we handle a major renovation, things like that. I think we should spend some time thinking about those things and maybe include them in a cohabitation agreement."

Or: "I have been thinking about the children, we have our work cut out for us blending that gang, we would benefit from spending some time thinking about how all that will work, including financial responsibilities. A cohabitation agreement might help."

Or: "I have been thinking about how we will manage our finances once we are under the same roof. Will we need a joint bank account? What about savings? RRSPs? We would benefit from a bit of planning and making sure we are on the same financial page. A cohabitation agreement might help us to do that."

None of the above answers sounds as if a threat to the relationship is being posed, but each response addresses the key question "Why do we need a cohabitation agreement?"

Do give yourself enough time.

Procrastination is something that will hurt the negotiation of an amicable cohabitation agreement. If there is a good reason to have a cohabitation agreement, then both partners will likely come to the same conclusion given enough time. If you are thinking about a cohabitation agreement, you may be well ahead of your partner on the subject. He or she will need time to catch up.

If you are planning to live together, then I suggest you have at least six months to move from a preliminary conversation about the need for a cohabitation agreement, to follow-up meetings where you gather and share information, to reviewing a draft cohabitation agreement, to making changes, and to consulting lawyers for independent legal advice. Hoping that all those steps can be achieved in a few weeks or few days is unrealistic. You need to give yourself and your partner enough time to work on this agreement.

You also need to give yourself lots of time to have the preliminary conversation. This isn't a conversation that is started unless you have time to get into some of the reasoning behind it immediately. I would set aside an hour to talk about some of the reasoning behind the need for a cohabitation agreement. This conversation is going to take place in a number of instalments and the very first instalment is critical to keeping you on a civil path. Find a quiet place to have the conversation where you will not be interrupted by business, a family, or children. But do be aware of things going on in your partner's life. We all lead busy lives and have many commitments and responsibilities. If he or she is in the middle of caring for an ill parent, transitioning to a new job, recovering from a layoff, or just preoccupied with important things in their life, make sure that you initiate this conversation at a time that is sensitive to their needs.

Do use the conversation as an opportunity to discuss the need for wills, powers of attorney, and insurance.

As you have seen from previous chapters, there is a lot more to cohabitation these days than simply moving in under the same roof. As people blend families and take responsibility for each other moving forward in their relationship, there are many other issues that need to be addressed. Common-law couples in particular require wills to deal with their estates. Powers of Attorney for Personal Care and for Property can make life a lot easier if there is a emergency that prevents someone from making decisions about their health and or their property. In addition, if it is a situation of dependency between two people, or a situation involving children, there may be a need to have a discussion about putting life insurance in place to protect each other and the family. Why not use the opportunity to discuss all of these issues at the same time. A cohabitation agreement can be made to work in conjunction with a person's will and powers of attorney.

Do keep it simple.

In this context I don't mean just keeping the conversation simple, I also mean making sure that you keep your eye on the ball for the purpose of the cohabitation agreement. There should be one or two justifications for requiring a cohabitation agreement. This should be enough to allow you to agree to continue having a discussion. Don't make the mistake of overwhelming your partner at this first meeting with all of the things you feel need to be set out in the cohabitation agreement; there will be lots of time to incorporate other details as you move forward.

In one case, a couple started their conversation about a cohabitation agreement on the basis that they were blending two families and moving into a home that had been previously owned by one of them; that's more than enough justification for a cohabitation agreement discussion. Unfortunately, they then went on to propose that the cohabitation agreement also micromanage their day-to-day living, including such things as household duties, yard work and other lifestyle "do's" and "don'ts." The discussion quickly went from looking like a cohabitation agreement to the design of a straight jacket, and they took a step back from the cohabitation. Keep the discussion simple and make sure that the cohabitation agreement solves problems and doesn't create them.

Do be fair and respectful.

As I have mentioned earlier, one person in the couple is usually far ahead of the other in the discussion of the need for a cohabitation agreement. It is a rare thing to hear someone say, "You know, I was thinking we needed a cohabitation agreement, too." Your partner may need time to come around to the idea and the justification for the agreement. That means being patient and being fair to allow your partner to digest the information that you are imparting.

These discussions can never be based on ultimatums or deadlines. It is one thing to set a timetable for moving forward with the discussion; it is quite another thing to tell somebody that if you don't hear the answer that you want to hear within seven days, then the cohabitation is off. If someone is in that position, they have probably not left themselves enough time to have the discussion properly and they are not being fair or respectful of their partner's need to understand the purpose of the cohabitation agreement.

~

Let's look at the other side of that conversation—things that can hurt the discussion.

THE "DON'TS"

The following are five things you should try to avoid as you begin this delicate discussion.

Don't present your partner with a draft contract.

Take a minute to put yourself in your partner's shoes. You have just been told that your partner wants to sit down and have a conversation about something that is very important. Your partner has set aside some time for a private conversation and there is a sense that it's important. He or she begins the conversation by saying, "I think we need a cohabitation agreement," and then presents you with a draft agreement for your review. What would you think about your partner suddenly presenting you with a draft agreement? First, you would think that your partner has been working on the agreement for many weeks or months without discussing it with you, which wouldn't get the conversation off to a very good start. Second, you would begin to wonder what else had been going on without your knowledge and you would feel a little bit suspicious. Third, you would feel that you are being presented with an ultimatum: "Sign this agreement or else." Presenting a draft contract does not produce warm and fuzzy feelings.

Don't mention lawyers.

In Chapter 9, "Signed, Sealed, and Delivered," we will be looking at the role of independent legal advice, and in Chapter 8, "The Role of Your Lawyer," we will be looking at a lawyer's guidance in the drafting of a cohabitation agreement. In your initial conversation with your partner, and in the early stages of discussing a cohabitation agreement, there is no need to mention that lawyers are or will be involved. In my experience the mention of lawyers being involved immediately gets everyone's back up and creates suspicion. It suggests that the legal wheels are already in motion and sends the message that your partner is way ahead of you in preparation of an important legal document.

Your initial conversations should be about the purpose of a cohabitation agreement, things that it can achieve for both of you, and how it might strengthen your relationship. There is more than enough information in this book for both of you to understand the answers to those questions without any mention of lawyers. Who knows? It may be possible for you to negotiate and conclude your agreement without the involvement of lawyers.

Don't rush the discussion.

Again, this is a simple reminder that one of you may be way ahead of the other in considering this a legal document and attempting to rush the discussion will only undermine the possibility of some goodwill at the outset.

Don't present a one-sided option.

This agreement has to be for the both of you. If the agreement that you describe to your partner at the outset is something that is designed solely to protect you, or your property, or your children, it may leave your partner wondering what's in it for them. If the agreement is about strengthening the relationship, why is only one half of the relationship mentioned in the option that you describe? Remember, this is to be a fair agreement and respectful of both your needs.

Don't blame it on other people.

The reason for a cohabitation agreement may very well be suggested by someone in your family or your legal advisor. For example, perhaps your family loaned you money to buy a home and that is the home in which you will cohabit. If your family is concerned that their loan needs to be protected, that is a good reason to consider a cohabitation agreement. That is quite different from a situation in which you open the discussion about a cohabitation agreement by suggesting the onus is on your family. "My parents will kill me if I don't guarantee them that their loan to me to buy this house is protected. They want me to have a cohabitation agreement." I think you will agree that that kind of opening line doesn't sound like a cohabitation agreement designed to strengthen your relationship, nor would an opening line that sounded like the following: "I met with my lawyer last week to finalize the divorce and he said that under no circumstances should you and I live together unless we have a cohabitation agreement."

Deflecting the desire for a cohabitation agreement away from yourself is only going to dilute any justification for the need for a cohabitation agreement. A better approach would be as follows: "We are going to be living in a home that I own, and the only reason I own it is because my parents loaned me money to assist in buying it. I want to make sure my parents are protected and that you and I understand how we are going to manage our life together in this house. I think a cohabitation agreement might help to make everyone feel more confident."

Or: "Now that I have the divorce finalized, I think it will be a great time for you and I to talk about how we're going to make sure we have a happy and strong relationship. One of the ways to put our minds at ease is to incorporate some basic financial understandings into a cohabitation agreement, especially around our home. We should also be thinking about Wills and Powers of Attorney to protect ourselves."

All of the above "do's" and "don'ts" will make your initial conversation, and the subsequent conversations, much easier.

WHAT IF YOU'RE ALREADY LIVING TOGETHER?

This will be a different conversation for one very simple reason: What happens if you do not agree about the need for a cohabitation agreement? If you have not yet reached the point in your cohabitation when rights and responsibilities have arisen, then you may be forced to consider ending the cohabitation or making some different choices about the issues that have given rise to the need for a cohabitation agreement. For example, let's consider Tom and Cindy. They have lived together for a year in a home that he owned before they met. They are about to undertake extensive renovations to his home. One possibility is that the renovation will be jointly funded. Tom is concerned about Cindy acquiring an interest in his home, simply by contributing to the renovations. Cindy is concerned about how her money is invested. Will she be compensated at some time for her investment in Tom's home, or will her investment be lost?

If Tom and Cindy are already cohabiting, what will happen if they cannot reach an agreement on the way in which they invest in Tom's home? They have three options:

1. Cindy will not invest in the renovations and Tom can either fund it alone or forego the renovations and they will continue to cohabit.
2. Tom and Cindy can end their relationship.
3. They can have a cohabitation agreement that addresses the issue that is of concern to both of them.

Having a conversation about a cohabitation agreement that involves the possibility of option two could have a chilling effect on the relationship. You will recall from the above section of "don'ts" that the presentation of an ultimatum is not a productive way to begin these discussions.

Consider another situation that is potentially even more explosive. Tom and Cindy have been living together for two-and-a-half years in Tom's house in Ontario. We know from Chapter 4 that if they separate after three years of cohabitation, then spousal support rights may arise for either of them. Cindy has indicated to Tom that she wants to leave her well-paying position to stay home and learn how to teach yoga. Her goal is to eventually open a yoga studio and give yoga classes in approximately three years. Tom and Cindy face a challenge. In six months (in Ontario at least), Tom may be responsible for paying Cindy's spousal support if the relationship ends. At this particular moment, six months prior to arrival of those rights and responsibilities they have three options:

1. Cindy does not make the career change and she continues to be able to support herself with her well-paying job.
2. Tom ends the relationship now before any support obligations to Cindy arise.
3. They sign a cohabitation agreement with respect to their own economic self-sufficiency and career plans and continue to cohabit.

As draconian as option 2 sounds, it at least gives Tom some control over his financial future and does not rule out the possibility of them restarting the relationship after they have a cohabitation agreement in place. In other words, they could end the relationship, terminate any obligations that Tom has been developing with respect to Cindy, negotiate a cohabitation agreement, and then start the cohabitation over again.

Consider another scenario for Tom and Cindy that is only slightly, but very importantly, different from the previous one. What if Cindy and Tom have been cohabitating for three-and-a-half years and spousal support obligations to Cindy may have already risen for Tom. Their options are:

1. Negotiate a cohabitation agreement and keep their relationship intact.
2. Cindy does not change careers and the problem is only deferred.
3. Tom ends the relationship and deals head on with the possibility that Cindy will seek spousal support from him. Experienced lawyers will tell Tom that it is better to deal with the possible claim for spousal support sooner rather than later—when Cindy is younger, when the relationship has only been a short one, and when she is better able to re-enter the work force with her skills.

~

With the above examples, I am illustrating the need for understanding your options if you are already cohabiting and want to have a conversation about a cohabitation agreement. Just because you know the options doesn't mean that you need to place them on the table at the opening of the discussion. Follow the same process of preparing for your meeting. Be able to explain why a cohabitation agreement is needed, and create options for dealing with your situation. Review all the "do's" and "don'ts" before your meeting and be realistic. If you see rights and responsibilities coming that you do not want, then be prepared to make tough choices, one of which may be termination of the relationship.

It should be clear by now that how you begin the conversation about a cohabitation agreement is critical. Second chances may be hard to come by, but if you remember some basic "do's" and "don'ts" it can be a successful beginning to a conversation that will last throughout your relationship. A good start will lead to a cohabitation agreement, a will, powers of attorney, a budget, financial planning, and enhanced respect and consideration for each other as partners.

Let's face it: in a successful, long-lasting relationship, you will have a lot to talk about and most of the "do's" and "don'ts" will continue to apply. So, whenever you have to have an important conversation in your relationship, do make a plan and have a purpose, do give yourself enough time, do keep it simple, do be fair and respectful, don't rush, don't be unfair, and don't deflect the onus from yourself.

8

THE ROLE OF YOUR LAWYER

In this chapter, I want to examine what some people consider the scariest part of discussing a cohabitation agreement—the prospect of having to hire a lawyer. And, yes, you may need a lawyer to help with this contract. I say "may need a lawyer" because it is possible to negotiate and sign this type of agreement without a lawyer—if you follow the rules and are fair with each other. There is no law in Canada that says independent legal advice (ILA) is mandatory for concluding a cohabitation agreement. However, ILA would be a nice safety net for a number of reasons and in this chapter we will consider the role of a lawyer in these agreements.

WHY DO PEOPLE FEAR HIRING A LAWYER?

The answer to this question is succinct: cost and control. Many people fear that once they hire a lawyer costs will spiral out of control, and that instead of the matter being a civilized and fair discussion between two people, it will become a war of letters and threats between lawyers. No one wants that kind of risk.

Cost

In some cases, lawyers charge their fees based on a block fee quoted at the outset (e.g., for a total of $3,000 I will do the following) or they will charge by the hour (e.g., $375 an hour times 10 hours equals $3,750 plus GST/HST). Lawyers chart out an hour that is broken into six-minute increments (or .1 of an hour). So, ten .1s equals 60 minutes. Every time a lawyer undertakes an action from answering a telephone call to preparing a letter, a record (called a "docket") is prepared and recorded in the office computer system or in your file. Most law firms use computerized docketing systems now that track everything from the length of a telephone call to the time required to prepare an agreement. The lawyer records his or her time and it accumulates until it is time to bill the client. If it takes a lawyer 10 hours to complete a particular service, he or she may simply multiply the number of hours by their hourly rate, make appropriate adjustments, add GST/HST and disbursements, and—voila—the client gets a bill. It is important in your initial conversation with a lawyer that you understand how fees and disbursements are treated. This will allow you to manage your cost from the outset. (We will be looking at tips for doing so in a moment.)

Control

The other fear of lawyers that clients have is loss of control of the conversation that started so beautifully and so diplomatically between the two of you. How can you ensure that the lawyers won't spoil this conversation? Again, this is a concern that must be dealt with from the initial conversation with the lawyers you chose.

Before we look at why you may need a lawyer, how to find the right one, and how to control the lawyer-client relationship, I want to share a little story with you about an unusual case.

A young couple wanted to negotiate a cohabitation agreement. They were getting ready to move into a property she owned. A four-way meeting was arranged between lawyers and clients. She was a young professional, a good saver from a good family, and going places. He was also a young professional and would tell anyone who would listen that he was going places, too. His family? Not so good with money. Him? Not so good with money. His personality? In a word, difficult. In any conversation about the cohabitation agreement, this young man was preoccupied with his future, his money, and his career. All of this became very clear during the meeting between lawyers and clients. As I watched the interaction between the clients, I was sure that I could see their future: ongoing battles about money, struggles for control, her continual management of his personality, and—for both of them—unhappiness. I suggested a break in the meeting and asked her privately, "Are you sure about this relationship?"

"Why?" she asked.

"Is this a life you are ready for? Are you prepared to manage his difficult personality throughout your relationship? We can see from even this preliminary meeting that he is a handful and focused on *his* future rather than *your* future as a couple."

I looked her straight in the eyes and said that based on my experience and my assessment of their relationship as a couple, I did not want to see her go down that path.

I mention this story because sometimes the lawyer-client relationship is about legal technicalities and preparation of documents, but sometimes there is the benefit of tapping into experience and insight, of having someone on your side who has seen many go before you. The right lawyer is there to provide you with as much guidance as he or she is providing technical services. The young woman called off the cohabitation and I think she made the right decision.

WHY DO YOU NEED A LAWYER?

Aside from providing the experience and guidance that I just described, when you hire a lawyer you are entering into a special relationship that is unlike any other. The solicitor-client relationship is special in that everything you tell your lawyer must remain confidential. Even a court cannot order a lawyer to divulge information that a client has shared with him or her. This confidentiality is critical to allowing a client to share everything without fear. This means that when you hire a lawyer to assist you with a cohabitation agreement, or any other legal service for that matter, you are free to treat the relationship as an opportunity to share information and explore questions that you may have without fear that it will be divulged.

When you hire a lawyer, one of the first steps that law firms undertake is to search their client list to ensure that there is no conflict of interest. The law firm wants to ensure that it can represent your interest in a way that is not in conflict with another client. For example, if a man and a woman need to negotiate a cohabitation agreement, but the law firm involved has represented the husband's business affairs, including financing to purchase property, the firm cannot represent the woman in the negotiation of the cohabitation agreement due to a conflict of interest.

Potential conflicts of interest are revealed by a search of the client list. Once it has been cleared for conflicts, the lawyer is free to open the file. The lawyer's primary function is to make sure any contract that is signed achieves goals for you in a cost-effective way. The lawyer's job is to ensure that you understand all of the options that are available, that you understand the advantages and disadvantages of various options, and that you make an informed choice when selecting an option to solve your particular need. It is your lawyer's job to ensure that you understand the consequences of *not* signing an agreement, as much as the consequences of signing one.

WHY DO YOU NEED A LAWYER WITH FAMILY LAW EXPERIENCE?

The lawyer who handled the purchase for sale of your home, who drafted your will, or who negotiated your employment contract, is probably not the lawyer who will look after your cohabitation agreement. That lawyer may be an excellent source of a referral for a lawyer with family law expertise, but he or she will not be going to prepare your cohabitation agreement.

As you can tell from the previous chapters, the rights and responsibilities of common-law couples across Canada vary from province to province and there is a specialized body of law that has accumulated around interpretation of those rights and responsibilities in our courts. You need a lawyer who understands the rights and responsibilities of common-law spouses. You are therefore looking for a lawyer who is a family law specialist or if not a specialist at least someone who devotes a large part of their practice to family law cases. The provincial law societies provide the names of lawyers who have special expertise in family law or who have a practice that is confined to family law. For example, in Ontario there are a number of practitioners who are certified as family law specialists. (See www.lsuc.on.ca)

In addition to having a lawyer who understands the rights and responsibilities of common-law spouses, you need a lawyer who is trained in the non-adversarial negotiation of cohabitation agreements. These lawyers may have even received training in mediation or collaborative family law. These are lawyers who are skilled in "diplomatic" negotiations. They understand that they have the task of protecting your rights but they also understand the importance of maintaining your relationship.

CHOOSING YOUR LAWYER AND MANAGING THE RELATIONSHIP

Your lawyer is going to ask you to sign a retainer, which is a contract by which you hire him or her. In the appendices, I have included a sample retainer so that you can see what these contracts look like. The retainer will set out the hourly rate of the lawyer, what service will be delivered on your behalf ("negotiate a cohabitation agreement"), the results that are expected, and an estimate of the amount of time that may be involved.

You will note from the retainer that I have provided in this book that an additional paragraph appears at the end of the second page. It caps the amount of legal fees that will be incurred unless your prior authorization is obtained first. This is a critical device that allows you to control the cost of these negotiations as well as control the relationship with your lawyer. You will recall the fear that I mentioned at the outset about costs spiraling out of control. This paragraph prevents that from happening.

It also provides an incentive to your lawyer to keep you informed about the state of negotiations and to manage his or her time effectively. Most good lawyers stay in regular contact with their clients, understand the budget that has been set for the negotiation of the cohabitation agreement, and work to bring the cohabitation agreement to a conclusion within that budget. However, there is a provision that

I recommend in all retainers, one that is important as a backstop protection for you: if it turns out that the fees and disbursements in the case are going to exceed the cap that has been set in the retainer, you have the option of increasing the cap and going forward, but you remain in control of the cost of the negotiation.

I also recommend to clients that at the outset they spend time getting to know the lawyer. At the initial meeting, treat this as a job interview. You are interviewing someone that you need to hire for an important job. Remember this: you are hiring the lawyer, not the other way around. I suggest speaking for at least 15 to 20 minutes with three experienced family law lawyers. Don't be shy about telling the lawyer that you only need to meet for a few minutes to discuss your case. Obviously the lawyer is not going to be able to give too much advice based on a short discussion, but you should be able to sense whether the comfort level is there for this important relationship.

You will want to ask the lawyer about his or her involvement in the negotiation and the drafting of the agreement. You do not want to meet an experienced senior lawyer only to find out that he or she hands the file to a junior lawyer whom you never meet. After 15 minutes you should be able to answer three questions:

1. Do I feel comfortable with this person?
2. Do I respect his or her opinion and experience?
3. Does he or she respect mine?

On the issue of junior lawyers being involved, I am not suggesting for a moment that they cannot provide a service to you as a client. In particular, if the senior lawyer can get a junior lawyer to do some of the background work and research at a lower hourly rate, this would be good for the bottom line in your case. However, in terms of the critical parts of your retainer, you want the lawyer that you have hired to be the one who does the negotiations, reviews the contract with you, and provides the advice about the options available to you.

In the retainer agreements that I have described above, you are hiring a lawyer to provide you with the advantages and disadvantages of various options. At the end of that exercise, a draft agreement will be presented to you. The lawyer will then be providing you with independent legal advice as to whether you should sign that agreement.

The lawyer is going to certify at the end of the agreement that he or she has reviewed it with you and that you have signed it voluntarily, that you understand your rights and responsibilities, that you have made full financial disclosure, and that you are signing the agreement voluntarily. The lawyer certifies the agreement. This certification or independent legal advice is considered important if a court later must assess whether this agreement should be enforced. Again, independent legal advice is not mandatory but it certainly sends a signal to the court that the agreement was negotiated and concluded in a way that meets a certain standard.

BUYING SOME ADVICE, BUT NOT INDEPENDENT LEGAL ADVICE

Not everyone can afford or wishes to have lawyers involved from start to finish in the negotiation of the cohabitation agreement. It is possible to simply buy advice from a lawyer as the negotiation progresses. Many lawyers are happy to meet with an individual to review the options that are available to the individual in the negotiation of the cohabitation agreement and some of the advantages and disadvantages. The client may have prepared a draft cohabitation agreement, assembled financial disclosure, and done some research on his or her own. It is quite possible to bring that material to an experienced family law lawyer and ask for a review to see if the client is on the right track. A lawyer in this situation will not provide independent legal advice or certify the cohabitation agreement once it is negotiated and signed, but it is possible to benefit from a lawyer's expertise from time to time as you negotiate the cohabitation agreement on your own.

USING A MEDIATOR

A mediator is a neutral third party who is trained to assist people in negotiations. The mediator does not impose a decision on the individuals who are negotiating. He or she simply assists them in reaching a concensus. The mediator is a neutral party; he or she is not biased in favour of one party or the other.

A mediator can be of use in the negotiation of a cohabitation agreement. Many family law lawyers are trained as mediators and it is possible to retain a family law lawyer/mediator to assist in the negotiations. This mediator will not be providing legal advice to either party, but may simply assist the couple in generating options that can be incorporated into the cohabitation agreement.

The family law lawyer/mediator may be of use where the issues concern property and finances as well as spousal support. Mediators who are trained as social workers, psychologists, or in other non-lawyer professions can be of assistance in the negotiations of issues concerning children.

The mediator will meet with you from time to time to discuss the options and to reach a consensus. At the end of the mediation, the mediator will provide a memorandum of understanding. That memorandum is then used to draft a cohabitation agreement. At that stage the couple can decide whether they wish to have independent legal advice about the agreement they negotiated with the mediator.

~

Finding the right lawyer, whether to provide you with independent legal advice or to simply provide you with legal advice from time to time while you negotiate yourself, is a critical step in moving the discussions forward in an amicable way that achieves the agreement you both seek.

9

SIGNED, SEALED, AND DELIVERED

The way in which a cohabitation agreement is created is very important. The provincial and territorial *Family Law Acts* stipulate that cohabitation agreements must have three key elements, as discussed below. In addition, the way in which the contract is negotiated and the circumstances under which it is signed are also critical to concluding an enforceable agreement. Let's consider these elements.

THE THREE "MUST-DO'S"

These three elements are easy but that doesn't mean they are not critical to having a valid agreement.

1. The agreement must be in writing.

A cohabitation agreement cannot be verbal or oral. It is common for couples to discuss some of what they would consider to be guidelines or understandings for their common-law relationship. If they choose to honour these understandings, there will be no dispute should the relationship break down. However, that is rarely the case. More often than not, the understanding has been forgotten, misunderstood, or one person simply decides not to honour it. Hence, the provision in provincial law that the agreements must be written. There is less likelihood of a disagreement if everything is written down, even if it is merely handwritten.

An instructive example of the need for a written agreement is the treatment of the *mahr* that is entered into before a Muslim marriage. The *mahr* is a verbal agreement entered into before the wedding as a form of marriage contract. A number of Canadian family law cases have considered this verbal religious tradition and found it unenforceable as a marriage contract under Canadian law.

When I say that the agreement must be in writing, that does not mean pages and pages of legalese; in one Alberta case the agreement was all of two lines, but it captured the intention of the parties and it was enforceable.

2. Both parties to the contract must sign it.

You will see from the example in Chapter 11 that the contract is signed on the last page. Lawyers will often have the parties to the contract initial each page as well as any changes that are made at the last minute. Uninitialled changes are unenforceable. This prevents any argument later about whether the page is an original or whether the handwritten change was agreed to by both parties. Now what would someone be thinking who tries to delete and replace pages of a signed agreement? Say it ain't so! As a precaution, lawyers always have the parties to a legal contract initial each page to mark them as a part of the final agreement.

There is no requirement that the cohabitation agreement be signed at the same time by each of the parties. More often than not, one party signs one day and then it is sent to the other side for review and the other party, if in agreement, then signs it. This can be relevant to the effective date of the contract. Most cohabitation agreements contain a paragraph which states that the agreement is effective the day upon which the last party signs it. This means that when a party signs the agreement, he or she should write down the date beside their signature. The cover page for the contract should also have a date on it. In this regard see the precedent in Chapter 11.

People sometimes ask lawyers at the time of signing their agreement, "How shall I sign it? Should I use my regular signature?" I think that what they really mean is, "Do I need to write my signature out exactly the way the name is typed in the agreement?" The answer is no; you should simply use your regular signature the same way in which you would sign a cheque or the back of your credit card.

3. Signatures must be witnessed.

A third party is needed to witness the signatures. Canadian courts have rejected agreements where the parties have witnessed each other's signatures. It is therefore advisable to have a separate witness for each signature, although one person can witness both signatures if absolutely necessary. The witness should also print their name and address under the signature. If they need to be located at a later date to verify their signature, it makes it easy to identify and locate them.

What is the purpose of the witness? The witness is simply attesting to the fact that the signature beside theirs is the signature of the person named in the contract. Ideally, if a stranger is asked to be a witness, then the person signing the contract should produce some identification to the witness to prove their identity and that it is indeed their contract. The witness is not vouching for any of the contents of the agreement and there is no need for the witness to review its contents prior to witnessing the agreement. The witness is not warranting that the person understands the agreement, or that they are even signing it voluntarily. That person is merely saying, "I saw Mr. or Ms._____ sign this agreement." The witness must also be present when the person signs the agreement. They cannot be presented with the signed contract and told, for example, "Oh, Erika signed this 30 minutes ago and had to leave, but you know it's her signature." This applies even if the witness knows that Erika signed it and knows that this is her signature. Since both people must be present at the time of signing and witnessing, the signature that is being witnessed must be an original. It cannot be a photocopy or fax.

The only exception to this rule that I have encountered is a British Columbia case where the wife did not sign the agreement at the same time as the witness, but then abided by the terms of the agreement for a period of time. In that case, the court felt it could enforce the terms of the agreement even though there was a defective signing of it. I don't think that we can rely on that case to protect improper witnessing of a contract, so follow the rules.

OBTAIN INDEPENDENT LEGAL ADVICE

In Chapter 8, we looked at the role of the lawyer in negotiating and signing a cohabitation agreement. Here I simply want to remind you that there is no law which requires Canadians to get a lawyer to sign off on one. So why are lawyers involved and what do they bring to the discussion?

For many years it was simply to make sure that the technical requirements were met, but as you can see from the foregoing paragraphs, those requirements are very straightforward: written, signed, and witnessed. Experienced lawyers will probe the financial disclosure made by each party to make sure a full picture is available to their client.

We saw in Chapter 8 that a lawyer's experience can have quite an impact in terms of whether this contract is personally good for the client. In other words, the lawyer can probe the client himself or herself. The lawyer can ask questions that can be answered confidentially when the client is away from family members, their spouse, or friends, who may be giving them unsolicited advice. The lawyer can ask: "Do you want this agreement?"; "Do you understand what you are doing?"; "Do you understand the implications in, say, ten years if you are, for example, signing a spousal support release?"; "Are you satisfied with this?"; "What if there are children born?"; "What if you lose your job?"; "Are you being pressured?" A lawyer can scratch at the surface to make sure that what lies beneath is true consent.

Involving a lawyer adds an extra layer of protection to the integrity of the agreement. A lawyer's job is much more than simply ensuring that it is written, signed, and witnessed. When the lawyer provides independent legal advice, he or she attaches a Certificate of Independent Legal Advice to the agreement verifying their work (see the precedent cohabitation agreement in Chapter 11). This certificate is a lawyer's statement that he or she took the client through the agreement, that the client understands the nature and consequences of the contract, that the client understands its purpose and is signing it voluntarily, that he or she is not being pressured, hoodwinked, tricked, or bamboozled in any way, and that the agreement appears to be fair for the client. That is what a good lawyer brings to the negotiation of a cohabitation agreement.

If a court is asked years later to throw out a cohabitation agreement, one of the first questions asked will be "Was there independent legal advice?" This does not mean that the court will automatically uphold every cohabitation agreement simply because a lawyer provided independent legal advice, but any lawyer trying to challenge a cohabitation agreement will have a tougher job if there has been meaningful independent legal advice provided. I say "meaningful" because we will see in the next section of this chapter that sometimes independent legal advice can be defective. However, if the lawyer who gave the independent legal advice is particularly well known in a community as an experienced and respective family law lawyer, then a challenge to the agreement is much less likely.

I have participated in meetings where a cohabitation agreement or marriage contract was being reviewed by lawyers with a view to challenging it. When it was revealed that a particularly well-respected lawyer had given the independent legal advice, the lawyers reviewing the contract said in unison, "Oh, it will never get thrown out!" End of discussion.

~

At the other end of the spectrum there are cases where one lawyer prepared the agreement in full and sent it to another lawyer for review. The lawyers who reviewed it barely spent any time with the client or analyzing the agreement. Later, when the cohabitation agreement was challenged, the judge called the independent legal advice "perfunctory at best." That contract was thrown out even though there was independent legal advice.

In one New Brunswick case, the judge who examined the circumstances under which the agreement was signed felt the legal advice was not adequate enough to overcome the wife's vulnerability and threw out the agreement. So as you can see, a lawyer's independent legal advice is not a bulletproof guarantee that the agreement will be upheld. However, done in the right way, with the right lawyer, it is a definite layer of protection if it is not just legal advice but *effective* legal advice.

DOING IT YOURSELF

Given the foregoing discussion, why not try and do the agreement yourself? As you can see, the technical requirements are straightforward. Yes, disclosure is of critical importance, but if you can assemble a full asset-and-liability picture and lay out all your financial cards on the table, it should not be an issue. You could even meet with a lawyer for a little advice just to make sure you are on the right track.

If you decide to do it yourself, what could possibly go wrong? Let's look at what some people did and how they ruined their cohabitation agreements. I'm sharing the following information with you not to discourage you from trying to design your own agreement, but to help you avoid some of the mistakes that others made. It is helpful to learn from their experiences.

How to Ruin Your Cohabitation Agreement

Before we examine some of the ways in which cohabitation agreements have been ruined, let's consider for a moment the context in which these agreements come under scrutiny. One of the most common contexts is where the relationship has ended and a dispute has arisen about property, children, or support, one party will wish to rely on the cohabitation agreement (after all, that's why it was drafted and signed) but the other party, for whatever reason, thinks the contract should not apply. Another context is in a situation where one spouse has passed away and a dispute over property or support has arisen in the context of interpreting their estate.

A typical example would be Jillian, a teacher, and Michael, an engineer. They lived together for 10 years but have split up over a dispute about children. Jillian thought they were going to start a family and get married, but Michael ultimately decided against it. They had signed a cohabitation agreement that they had drafted themselves. Each, it was agreed, would keep their own property as it was brought into the relationship and as it was acquired during the relationship. There would be no spousal support if they separated. It seemed like a good idea at the time because they were both financially independent, but now Jillian is out of work because they moved to a small town where Michael took up a new position with a mining company, and Jillian has only been able to get part-time work as a substitute teacher.

When they arrived in the town, they bought a house but it is registered in Michael's name only as he was the one who put down the deposit.

Jillian has consulted a lawyer and he suggests that the cohabitation agreement be scrutinized to see if there are any grounds for setting it aside. My point here is that the contracts are attacked in unpleasant circumstances when the parties' needs are different. Memories change, attitudes are different, feelings may be hurt, people are often angry. All of this could be just as true if, in the above example, Michael had died without a will or perhaps had left everything in a will to someone other than Jillian. The feelings could be intense and her needs very great in a small town with no way to support herself. Jillian's lawyer, after reviewing the technical requirements around the execution of the cohabitation agreement, would then consider the typical grounds for attacking a contract. Let's look at those typical grounds.

One of the parties failed to make a full financial disclosure.

In order for the two people affected by this contract to be genuinely and fairly entering into it, everything must be on the table. They must know everything about each other's financial situation—good and bad. They must know all of the other person's assets, the value of those assets and the extent of that person's liabilities. When a court is asked at a later date to assess the fairness of a contract, the judge starts with the adequacy of financial disclosure. In Ontario, Section 56(4) of the *Family Law Act* states: "56. (4) A Court may set aside a domestic contract or a provision in it, if a party failed to disclose to the other significant assets or significant debts or other liabilities existing when the domestic contract was made."

This idea of disclosure was brought into dramatic focus in a case called *LeVan v. LeVan*. Let's look at the situation they encountered. The LeVan marriage lasted only seven years and when the couple separated in October of 2003, she was 42 years old and he was 44.

They had had two children who were now six and eight as of the date of separation. Ms. LeVan had an Honours BA in psychology and a teacher's certificate; Mr. LeVan, on the other hand, had a diploma in business marketing. Once the children were born, Ms. LeVan became a stay-at-home mom and Mr. LeVan, along with other members of his family, owned the majority of shares in a company called Westcast Industries Inc., which was the largest manufacturer of exhaust manifolds in the world and a publicly traded company. At the time of the marriage in 1996, Ms. LeVan was earning approximately $13,000 a year and Mr. LeVan $52,000.

Mr. LeVan's father had built Westcast into the world's largest supplier of auto parts and he and his wife, Mr. LeVan's mother, with help from corporate and financial advisors, had created a complex corporate structure that included several companies and a family trust. Mr. LeVan's father wanted to protect his son's shares in Westcast in the hope that he and his wife and their four children, including Mr. LeVan, would always maintain control of Westcast.

It was clear from the outset that Ms. LeVan was aware that she would be asked to sign a marriage contract. Her evidence at trial was that even before they got engaged, her husband told her that his family would require her to sign a marriage contract to exclude any interest in the Westcast shares. It was even discussed at the family dinner table with Mr. LeVan's parents. Mr. LeVan's father took the initiative and contacted a lawyer to prepare a draft marriage contract dealing with spousal support and protection of the shares in Westcast. Mr. LeVan ended up meeting with a lawyer at a large Toronto law firm and a draft marriage contract was completed. Ms. LeVan hired a lawyer who was a general practitioner in a small town in Ontario. That lawyer estimated that he spent about 40 percent to 50 percent of his practice in the area of family law.

Attached to the draft marriage contract were schedules that set out a list of significant assets and significant debts. They disclosed Mr. LeVan's net worth as being "$80,000 plus LeVan family companies' interest." No values were inserted for such things as his RRSPs, bank accounts, or the values in the LeVan companies. The lawyer for Mr. LeVan, when she was called as a witness at the trial, acknowledged that it was essential that the other side know Mr. LeVan's actual income and actual net worth, but she did not provide that information to the wife's lawyer other than as set out in Schedule A attached to the draft agreement. She herself did not have a full grasp of Mr. LeVan's net worth which, it turns out, was approximately $14 million. By the time of separation, Mr. LeVan was worth **considerably more** and Ms. LeVan had signed a marriage contract releasing any interest in those assets and releasing any entitlement to spousal support. She did so by signing a marriage contract less than a month before the wedding having been told that if she did not sign the contract there would be no wedding.

To make matters more complicated, the wife changed lawyers prior to signing the agreement. When her first lawyer attempted to obtain more financial disclosure, he was rebuffed; when he gave advice to Ms. LeVan and made enquiries of the husband's lawyer for further disclosure, Mr. LeVan's lawyer told Mr. LeVan that, in her opinion, she did not think the lawyer representing his wife knew what he was doing. When Mr. LeVan then told his wife that her lawyer was incompetent and "an idiot," she was driven to find a new lawyer. Guess what? The new lawyer Ms. Levan was referred to, and hired, had acted for the husband's lawyer in her own divorce a few months earlier.

The wedding was now only a week away and the pressure was on to sign a contract. The wife's second lawyer did not request any further disclosure and met with the wife for approximately one hour. Some minor amendments were requested which were considered inconsequential by the husband's lawyer; the contract was quickly signed and the wife, under considerable pressure, two days before the wedding, still felt that there would be no wedding without a marriage contract being signed.

When the parties later separated and the wife learned the consequence, her new lawyer suggested that she ask the court to throw out the agreement because there was inadequate financial disclosure, and the advice that she had received from her previous two lawyers was not effective independent legal advice.

In the *LeVan* decision, the trial judge threw out the marriage contract, both as it related to support and division of assets, and made an award in favour of the wife in the amount of $5.3 million, not quite what was expected by Mr. LeVan and his parents.

In cases involving valuable or extensive assets, the need for financial disclosure, particularly after the *LeVan* decision, has resulted in lawyers exchanging thick briefs of documents with copies of supporting ownership materials, valuations, appraisals, and other forms of backup documentation for all assets and liabilities of each party. Income disclosure includes copies of income-tax returns and backup documents for all sources of income. Accountants are sometimes involved to explain the corporate holdings of the parties. This disclosure, before signing, must also be mindful of what may happen in the future to the people involved: How old are they? When will they retire? What are their career expectations? Will there be children? Will someone move their residence to join the relationship? Will one party move their children from, say, Toronto to Vancouver? How will they be supported? And so on.

Many, many questions are asked as a part of proper financial disclosure. You will see in the sample cohabitation agreement provided in Chapter 11, the parties warrant to each other that they have made full disclosure to each other and that they are each satisfied with the disclosure. Hiding an asset, overvaluing an asset, undervaluing an asset, or not being open and honest about significant assets and liabilities may well provide an excuse to invalidate the entire agreement at a later date.

In most cases, though, the cohabiting couple may have modest assets, a home, a recreational property, vehicles, some retirement savings, a pension, furniture, and so on. A forensic audit of values and liabilities would be disproportionate to the value of the assets and liabilities in question. In such cases, disclosure is made by the parties and an opportunity to investigate further is presented. If the people are satisfied with the information and trust each other, they may simply attach to the cohabitation agreement two schedules of assets and liabilities disclosing each other's net worth and income. In the agreement they warrant to each other that the disclosure has been adequate and that they accept it without further investigation.

Someone didn't understand the nature and consequences of the contract.

For a contract to be valid, the person signing it must understand the character of the document as well as the impact that it's going to have on their life. There is a strong connection between obtaining independent legal advice and understanding the nature and consequences of the contract. As I mentioned earlier, this is often what a lawyer brings to the table. The lawyer and client will spend a good deal of time going through a list of "what ifs" what if you have children; what if you lose your job; what if you move; what if someone dies; what if you become sick; and so on and so on. In each set of circumstances, the lawyer and client review the impact of the contract on those circumstances. By reviewing the details, the client comes to appreciate exactly what the impact of the contract will be.

Returning to the LeVan case, Ms. LeVan was surprised to learn, after separation, that not only had she excluded an interest in the value of Mr. LeVan's shares as of the date of marriage, but she had also excluded any interest in the growth in the value of those shares over the course of the marriage. Proper legal advice would have disclosed this important consequence of the contract. As you can see, there is a strong relationship between independent legal advice and financial disclosure. Is it possible for someone to understand the nature and consequences of a contract if they do not have adequate financial disclosure? Probably not. Mr. LeVan was relying on the fact that his wife-to-be knew all along that she would be excluded from having any interest in his family's business. After all, what more did she need to know? Whether he was worth $14 million or $30 million at the time of marriage, she would have signed the same agreement. Reliance on that kind of understanding of the nature and consequences of the contract was not good enough for the judge in *LeVan* and shouldn't be good enough for you in doing your cohabitation agreement.

Someone made a misrepresentation about the contract.

A misrepresentation is a statement that is untrue about the factual basis for requiring a cohabitation agreement or, similarly, not revealing a fact that is important to a person's understanding of the requirement for a contract.

Consider, for example, the situation in which James and Bobbi prepare to cohabit. If James told Bobbi that a cohabitation agreement was required because his business partners required him to exclude any interest a common-law spouse may have in their company, then this is an inaccurate reason for Bobbi to sign. Common-law spouses, we have seen, do not have an automatic interest in each other's property. For James to tell her that his partners require her to sign the agreement is a misrepresentation. Bobbi has relied on that essential fact in agreeing to sign the contract. If they later separate and that misrepresentation is disclosed, a court will have an excellent reason to throw out the contract. In a way, misrepresentation is connected to understanding the nature and consequences of the contract. Can someone understand what a contract is going to do if the very basis for the need for a contract has been misrepresented to them? Probably not.

Someone made a mistake.

This is similar to a misrepresentation but the mistake need not be the fault of a party to the agreement. For example, if a common-law spouse was under the mistaken impression that a cohabitation agreement had to be signed in order to immigrate to Canada, which is not the case, then the basis for them signing the agreement is mistaken. The mistake, whether honest or induced, is a belief that a fact is true when it is not. If such a mistaken belief comes to light, the court will have an excellent excuse to interfere with the contract and perhaps set it aside.

Someone was under undue influence or duress.

The *Family Law Act* of each province and territory provides that a court may set aside a cohabitation agreement, or even a provision in a cohabitation agreement, if the contract or the provision is not in accordance with the general law of contract. This means that all of the other reasons for attacking contracts can be employed against a cohabitation agreement.

A typical ground for attacking a contract is that the person who signed it did not do so willingly. In other words, that person was forced or coerced into signing the agreement. It doesn't need to be as dramatic as the infamous *Godfather* scene in which "someone made him an offer he couldn't refuse"; it can, in fact, be quite subtle. For example, in a Canadian case in which a common-law wife relied upon her common-law husband for all business and financial decisions, and did so throughout the negotiation of a cohabitation agreement, a court ultimately found that the husband exercised undue influence over the wife by virtue of the dramatic difference in the balance of power between them.

Other examples of undue influence or duress include situations similar to that which we saw in the LeVan case, where the husband told the wife repeatedly in the days leading up to the wedding that if the marriage contract was not signed, there would be no wedding at all. In another case, the person presented with a cohabitation agreement was told that if she did not sign it, the family would be extremely angry with her.

When the courts have been asked to look at a situation of alleged undue influence or duress, it has come down to a consideration of the ability of one spouse to dominate the will of the other, whether through manipulation, coercion or use of power. Imagine for a moment the pressure faced by a young woman who is expecting a child and is then presented with a "take it or leave it" cohabitation agreement; if she signs it, she and the child's father will cohabit; if she does not sign it, she will be on her own and likely involved in a claim for child support and custody. The court will not enforce cohabitation agreements entered into under situations that involve violence, threats, intimidation, economic duress, or oppression.

Someone commits a fraud.

This is very similar to a misrepresentation except that, in the case of fraud, the person making the misrepresentation has every intention of taking something from the other party to which they are not entitled. Imagine a situation where a husband has a number of documents prepared including real estate transactions, corporate bylaws, and other materials but slips into the pile of documents to be signed a cohabitation agreement in which the wife transfers all interest in her property to the husband. Similarly, consider the situation that I mentioned earlier where one party tried to change pages in the document after it had been signed. Those are good examples of fraud and a court will obviously throw out any agreement reached under such circumstances.

The contract is unconscionable or unfair.

This is a relatively new development in the area of attacking cohabitation agreements. In the past, the courts were reluctant to spend too much time evaluating the relative advantages and disadvantages of the deal for the parties involved. The court was generally concerned only with whether the contract met its technical requirements and whether it was valid under the general law of contract. In other words, as long as it was signed properly, and proper disclosure had been made, and no one was acting under duress, then the contract would be enforceable. However, over time as courts were invited in to examine the circumstances under which the contract was signed and whether there was undue influence or duress, it also started to consider whether the deal was fair or not. Unconscionability—which means a situation that is grossly unfair—occurs generally in situations where there is inequality between the people signing the contract and an improvident outcome for one of them. Both must be present; in other words, if there are two parties involved in the negotiation of the contract and they are of equal bargaining power but happen to arrive at a bad deal, the court will not be interested in disturbing that contract. However, if there is an inequality of bargaining power between the two parties and it appears that one party was preying on the other, that they used their advantage to obtain the other party's signature on an improvident contract, then the court will be prepared to intervene.

In the context of unconscionability, effective independent legal advice should be more than enough to overcome problems of unequal bargaining power and improvident deals.

Someone repudiates the contract.

Repudiation of a contract means that a party has refused to abide by the contract. That person's repudiation of it disentitles them from enforcing the contract against the other party. Imagine a situation in which a man and a woman enter into a cohabitation agreement in which the man agrees to support the woman's children and pay for their attendance at private school. On this understanding, she moves the children from their schools in one city to private schools in the city in which the common-law partner resides. Imagine, too, that this cohabitation agreement includes a release of any spousal support. If the children are moved and the common-law partner then refuses to pay for the private schooling for the children and the relationship breaks down, a court will not allow the man to enforce the spousal support release against her as he has repudiated the contract. Court cases that have examined situations like this sometimes talk about the occurrence of a "fundamental breach" of the contract. A fundamental breach is one that deprives the innocent party of substantially the entire benefit of the contract into which they entered.

A provision is not in the best interests of the children.

The courts always reserve the right to protect the interest of children. If a provision in a cohabitation agreement is considered to not be in the best interests of the children, or, for example, is not considered to be in accordance with the Child Support Guidelines, then the court will set aside that provision of the contract and do what it considers to be right for the children. Consider, for example, a couple who agrees that if the relationship does not work out when they begin to cohabit, the maximum amount of income that will be considered in calculating child support under the Child Support Guidelines will be $100,000. If at the time of separation the party who would otherwise be paying child support earns in excess of $100,000, the court will not be bound by the agreement to artificially lower the income.

Onus

Assuming that one party believes that he or she is in a position to attack the cohabitation agreement, that person should also be aware of the approach that is taken by a court. It is not enough to simply make an allegation, for example, that one suffered duress when signing the agreement. The court has made it clear that when challenging an agreement, the party who wishes to set it aside must first show that he or she fits within one of the grounds for attacking the agreement. So, in the example of duress, the person attacking the cohabitation agreement must convince the court that he or she was indeed threatened with negative consequences for not undertaking to sign the agreement. If the court accepts that evidence, it then goes on to consider a second aspect. The person attacking the agreement must then persuade the court to exercise its discretion to set aside the agreement. The onus is on the person attacking the agreement to convince the court that it should use its discretion to help him or her.

What is the Supreme Court of Canada's attitude to cohabitation agreements?

Marriage contracts and cohabitation agreements are treated virtually identically by the courts. The Supreme Court of Canada, in a case that involved a battle between two lawyers who were married to each other, noted that there were no hard and fast rules about giving deference to one form of contract over another. But the court did have the following to say about marriage contracts and I believe that these words apply equally to cohabitation agreements:

> In some cases, marriage contracts ought to be accorded a greater degree of defence than separation agreements. Marriage agreements define the parties' expectations from the outset, usually before any rights are vested and before any entitlement arises. Often, perhaps most often, a desire to protect pre-acquired assets or an anticipated inheritance for children of a previous marriage will be the impetus for such an agreement.

On the other hand marriage agreements may be accorded less deference because they are anticipatory and may not fairly take into account the financial means, needs, or other circumstances of the parties at the time of a marriage breakdown. The courts have an open mind when considering the enforceability of these agreements.

SOME TIPS FOR NEGOTIATING AND DRAFTING COHABITATION AGREEMENTS

- Avoid the appearance that one party is steering the other party to a particular lawyer for independent legal advice. While a spouse may simply be trying to be helpful and trying to speed the process along, to an outside observer it may appear that the legal advice received was not truly independent. The best advice is to simply ensure that they go to an experienced family law lawyer of their choice.
- As should be clear from the foregoing section about financial disclosure, make sure the disclosure is complete, accurate, and timely. If the assets and their values involve corporate holdings, for example, provide a flow chart that shows the relationship between the companies. Simply providing a stack of incomprehensible documents will not be considered adequate financial disclosure at a later date.
- Use language that can be understood. There's no need to overcomplicate matters with a lot of legalese and mumbo jumbo. Write it in a language that both parties can understand. It is interesting to note that in the LeVan case discussed earlier it was clear from the evidence at trial that, not only did the spouses not understand the contract, neither did the lawyers nor some of the valuators who were called as expert witnesses at trial. That is a bad sign.
- Remember to ensure that each person has adequate time to review the contract, make suggestions, review disclosure, get advice and actually feel like they have a hand in the design of this important agreement.
- Avoid negotiating a contract that is simply a blanket waiver of all claims. If you're going to the trouble of negotiating a cohabitation agreement, take the time to tailor the agreement to accomplish something that strengthens the relationship. Simply making blanket waivers may be an invitation at a later date to think of the contract as being unconscionable or unfair to one of the parties.
- Be aware that lawyers are wary of participating in the negotiation of cohabitation agreements and marriage contracts. No one wants to be in the position of the two lawyers for the wife in *LeVan*

where they were criticized for not having scrutinized the financial disclosure sufficiently. Often clients will contact the lawyer's office and ask to meet to discuss a marriage contract or cohabitation agreement. Their first question is "Do you have experience in this area?", and the second question is, "How much will this cost?" In most cases an experienced lawyer is unable to provide an estimate, because he or she has no idea what will be involved. Even after a first meeting with a client, an estimate will be difficult until financial disclosure is produced. As the time and fees involved climb, the client often balks at the potential bill that is being incurred and pressures the lawyer to speed through their analysis. In many cases a wedding is looming and there is pressure to make sure that the contract is signed. No one wants to spoil the party. The reason I mention this, is that lawyers often would rather simply avoid providing independent legal advice on these contracts because the fees that are charged are often out of proportion to the potential liability that is taken on.

- For example, in one Ontario case, the lawyer who represented the husband was sued on the basis that he did not protect the wife's interests. I know that sounds strange, but it took a Superior Court judge to decide that the lawyer who is negotiating a cohabitation agreement or marriage contract does not owe a duty to protect the opposite side in the family law dispute. In that particular case, when the contract was thrown out, it proved costly for the husband. The question that arose was did the husband's lawyer have an obligation to make sure that the contract was fair to the wife and in doing so, thereby protect the husband and the agreement from attack at a later date.

It is a tricky business providing Independent Legal Advice, especially if a contract is set aside by the court and hundreds of thousands of dollars or even of millions of dollars suddenly change hands.

All of these rules and guidelines for preparation, signing, and negotiation of cohabitation agreements are designed for a reason. No one wants to see a spouse taken advantage of; no one wants to have contracts signed under circumstances that create confusion and litigation at a later date. Contracts should be clear. They should say what they mean. They should achieve the intentions and goals of the people who sign the contract. Contracts should be fair to both spouses. They should have a purpose. They should strengthen the relationship, not create resentment or anxiety while the relationship is underway. If you keep the overriding goal of fairness in mind and follow the rules set out above, you will have a much greater chance of your marriage contract or cohabitation agreement surviving a challenge at a later date.

10

SAME-SEX COUPLES

Same-sex couples in Canada now enjoy the same rights and responsibilities as common-law couples and married couples, and protocols should a same-sex couple separate or should one of the partners die are virtually identical. They may enter into cohabitation agreements and marriage contracts and customize their rights and responsibilities. There are, however, some extra challenges that may be faced by same-sex couples and, in this chapter, we consider those challenges and some options for addressing them.

GETTING MARRIED IS THE EASY PART

Although this book is concerned with common-law couples, I thought I would add a few words about the impact of marriage rights on same-sex couples. Since approximately 2003, same-sex couples have had the right to marry in Canada. I was fortunate to be able to attend the first same-sex marriage in Canada, which occurred in the hallway at a courthouse on University Avenue in Toronto (the wedding occurred in the hallway because no cameras are allowed in courtrooms in Canada, and there were lots of pictures being taken). Marriage for same-sex couples now is the easy part. Divorce, however, in some cases, is not so easy if the couple leaves Canada after the wedding and then later attempts to divorce. Other jurisdictions, notably in the United States, do not recognize the the same-sex couple's marriage, so the foreign divorce laws are not available to the couple.

One option for the couple is to include a term in a marriage contract binding them to the laws of a Canadian province, in the event of a separation and divorce. This may assist the couple, should they be forced to return to Canada for a divorce at a later date. The key problem, however, is that our divorce laws require a period of residency prior to the issuance of a divorce application. If the couple has not actually resided in the province prior to applying for the divorce, then it may be rejected. The only solution in the long term is for more jurisdictions to expand the recognition of Canadian marriages for the purpose of divorce, whether the jurisdiction itself recognizes same-sex marriage.

SPERM DONATION

Fertility clinics use questionnaires to screen sperm donors. These questionnaires effectively block gay and bisexual men from donating sperm based on health and safety concerns about statistically higher risk of HIV. However, this may even occur when the person wishing to receive the donation already knows the donor. The clinics do not appear at this time to take the sperm donation on a client by client basis, but instead rely on a general exclusion of that population. This has led to the use of "do it yourself" techniques in the gay and lesbian community and the use of sperm donor contracts between gay donor men and lesbian mothers. Are these contracts enforceable? That is unclear at this stage, but as we will see in the next section, same-sex families can get crowded.

SAME-SEX FAMILIES, ADOPTION, AND SPERM DONORS

If a lesbian couple uses a sperm donation and a child is born, who is legally entitled to call themselves a parent? Certainly, the biological mother and the biological father have legal status (if the sperm donor is identifiable). But does the non-biological lesbian partner of the biological mother also have parenting rights? If she does, is it possible for the child who was born to have three parents, all recognizable as having parental status? The answer is yes. As a result of a court decision in Ontario in 2006, it is possible for a lesbian couple and the sperm donor to form a three-parent family.

In some families the non-biological parent may wish to adopt the child that was born. However, because of our adoption laws, adoption can extinguish the parental rights of someone such as a sperm donor who may wish to remain involved with the child. These kinds of issues can be addressed in a sperm donation contract, particularly if the donor of the sperm wishes to stay involved in the child's life and perhaps even be considered a parent. It is an area of the law that involves a great deal of uncertainty at this time.

TRANSGENDERING

This issue has, to my knowledge, only arisen once, but concerned the impact of a sex reassignment by a parent on their entitlement to claim custody of or access to a child. In this particular case, a Canadian went through a sex reassignment process that would transform them from the male to the female sex. The female ex-partner of this individual argued in court that the sex reassignment undermined that former father's ability to act as a parent. The court examined the child's best interests and came to the conclusion that the parenting would not be affected by the sex reassignment. An unusual situation, but a cogent reminder that the court is really only concerned with the child's best interests when issues—even as unusual as this one—arise.

Issues concerning same-sex couples and Canadian family law continue to emerge. It is an area being followed closely by lawyers and the courts.

11

LET'S LOOK AT AN ANNOTATED COHABITATION AGREEMENT

In this chapter I have set out an entire draft cohabitation agreement. Throughout the agreement I have inserted, from time to time, explanations about particular words or paragraphs to help you understand the purpose of that particular provision.

You will recall from Chapter 6, "Creating Your Own Set of Rights and Obligations," that as a couple you are free to include any terms you wish with respect to your property, spousal support, the day-to-day relationship, education and moral training of children, and any other matter related to your personal situation. However, you cannot include provisions that dictate custody of, and access to children, if and when they are born, or if and when you separate.

You will also recall that the court always reserves the right to disregard any provision not considered to be in the best interests of children. Similarly, any provision that tries to limit or eliminate an obligation to support a child will be disregarded by the court.

The following draft presents a sample agreement that includes some of the clauses that would be included in a basic agreement.

My annotations appear in italics. I hope a review of the draft and my comments help to promote questions and to focus your attention on clauses that might help you come to an agreement that suits both your needs.

COHABITATION AGREEMENT

It seems like a simple point, but it is important to name the document as a "Cohabitation Agreement." This will prevent an argument at a later date that one of the parties to the agreement did not understand what he or she was signing. In at least one case, one of the common-law partners tried to characterize a promissory note and a mortgage as the equivalent of a cohabitation agreement. The last thing you want to do is pay lawyers to fight over whether or not you actually signed a cohabitation agreement.

THIS Cohabitation Agreement made this ____________ day of ____________, 20___.

It is a small point, but you would be surprised how many people forget to put a date on the document. Unless you state otherwise somewhere in the agreement, such as on the signature page, this will be the date upon which the agreement comes into force.

BETWEEN:

This part of the cohabitation agreement is designed to set out who is entering into the agreement. It doesn't matter whose name appears first, but it does matter that you set out your correct legal names. A cohabitation agreement is a contract and in this area you are setting out the parties to the contract.

____

(referred to as "____________")

and

____

(referred to as "____________")

WHEREAS:

Using the word "whereas" sounds a little legalistic, but it really is meant to say "this is the background to why we are entering into this contract." In these paragraphs you have an opportunity to set out details about the background of your relationship and matters that are of importance to why you are entering into the agreement. In this section you can include, for example, your ages, your birthdates, the names of children who are affected by the agreement, details of previous marriages and divorces, and, importantly, to say plainly what you are trying to achieve by having a cohabitation agreement.

You will recall from Chapter 3, "Rights and Responsibilities to Each Other While Living Together," that it can be difficult to recall the actual moment that your cohabitation began. In this subparagraph you have an opportunity to set out specifically the date upon which the cohabitation began.

There was an interesting case in Nova Scotia in which a man and a woman separated after living together for about three years in a common-law relationship. The man had been hired on a six-month probationary contract to be the chief of a fire department and he needed to move to a new community and he did so, renting a fully furnished apartment while he waited to see if the probationary contract would become permanent.

Unfortunately, his common-law wife learned that he had been in a relationship with another woman and some discussions arose about whether she would join him even if the job became permanent. They sat down and negotiated a document in which he promised to pay to her $15,000 if and when he sold his home.

Later, his common-law wife refused to move to the new community and live with him and he contested his obligation to pay her $15,000 upon the sale of the home. He did so on the basis that there had been a misunderstanding about the circumstances under which

$15,000 was to be paid. He thought he only had to pay if she moved with him.

This problem, which had to be litigated in a costly way in the courts, could have been avoided with some clearer paragraphs in the "whereas" section.

So when you are drafting your cohabitation agreement take a few moments to write down exactly what it is you hope to achieve by the cohabitation agreement and include those words in this section.

(a) the parties intend to cohabit with one another commencing on ___________ or have been cohabiting since _________________;
(b) the parties intend this Cohabitation Agreement to provide for their respective rights and obligations during cohabitation or on ceasing to cohabit or on death;
(c) such rights and obligations (insert: *include ownership in or division of property, support obligations, and the right to direct the educational and moral training of their children.*)

NOW THEREFORE in consideration of the mutual covenants contained in this Agreement the parties agree as follows:

A cohabitation agreement is a contract. In order to have a contract three things need to be present:

(1) Someone needs to offer to do something;
(2) Someone needs to accept the offer;
(3) There needs to be some consideration or thing of value that passes between the two parties to the contract in order to seal the bargain.

In some agreements parties will put "in consideration of the payment of One Dollar ($1) the parties agree as follows." In this particular draft cohabitation agreement, the thing of value that is being exchanged between the parties—the consideration—are their promises and covenants to each other. I have never liked the idea of saying that a dollar seals the deal. I think the value of a cohabitation agreement is the mutual promises the individuals are making to each other.

SEPARATION AGREEMENT WITH FORMER SPOUSE (IF THIS APPLIES)

If there are some previous obligations to a spouse and/or children, this should be set out early on in the cohabitation agreement as a form of disclosure of existing commitments, and as recognition of both parties to the cohabitation agreement that these obligations exist.

The paragraph above is very basic. In some cases it may be advisable to set out some of the important details of that separation agreement or even consider adding it as a schedule to the cohabitation agreement. In that way there can be no misunderstanding about the disclosure by the party who has those existing rights and obligations.

1. ____________ entered into a written Separation Agreement with his/her former spouse dated ________________, and has transferred all property and paid all sums required to be transferred or paid by him prior to the date of this Agreement.

OWNERSHIP AND DIVISION OF PROPERTY

Statement of Assets and Liabilities

2. The parties each have assets acquired prior to the date of this Agreement and although each party has had an opportunity to investigate, examine, and appraise the value of the assets of both parties and the quantum of the liabilities of both parties, neither party wishes to do so.

a) ____________ represents that Schedule ___ contains a complete and accurate disclosure of all property registered in his/her name or of which he is the beneficial owner and of all debts whether presently owed or contingent.

b) ____________ represents that Schedule ___ contains a complete and accurate disclosure of all property registered in his/her name or of which she is the beneficial owner and of all debts whether presently owned or contingent.

You will recall from Chapter 6, "Creating Your Own Set of Rights and Obligations," that identification of assets that are not to be shared or assets that are being brought into the relationship is extremely important..

In the appendices, I have set out some work sheets and draft schedules to assist you in identifying and setting out your assets and liabilities as well as the value of those assets and liabilities. You will also recall from Chapter 9, "Signed, Sealed, and Delivered," the technical rules for making a cohabitation agreement that will stand up, that financial disclosure is critical to developing an enforceable contract. This disclosure is to be summarized in these schedules.

Classes of Property to Remain Separate

3. The following property, which is referred to collectively as "Independent Property" shall be and remain the sole and exclusive property of the other party throughout the period the parties cohabit and in the event that they cease to cohabit and upon the death of either party.

Note that this paragraph does two things:

(1) It sets out a category of property that will not be shared (referred to as "independent property.")
(2) It also says that that category of property will be the sole and exclusive property of that particular party while the couple is together, if they separate, or if one of them dies.

The following paragraph sets out exceptions to the general rule that independent property will not be shared.

4. Subject to clause 1(c), neither party shall under any circumstances acquire any interest in "Independent Property":

a) all real and personal property of the other party as described in Schedule "__" hereto;

b) all other real and personal property acquired by the other party prior to the date of this Agreement;

c) all real and personal property acquired by the other party in his or her name alone and after the date of this Agreement;
d) all income derived by the other party from any source;
e) all gifts acquired by the other party from any source;
f) all property received by the other party as damages; and
g) all real and personal property inherited by the other party;

In this paragraph the parties are saying to each other that here are specific categories of property that we will not be sharing with each other:

(1) Property that is set out in Schedules A and B
(2) Property that was owned prior to the date of the agreement (which should be set out in the Schedules)
(3) Property that was purchased or acquired in a person's name alone after the date of the agreement. (in other words, RSPs or title to a property in that person's name alone)
(4) Any income they get from any source (this could be employment income, investment income, rental income)
(5) All gifts acquired from any source (this could include gifts from family members, friends or business partners)
(6) Property received as damages (this could include money that someone receives because they were in a car accident or injured on the job)
(7) Any property that is inherited by the person (this could be property that is inherited by virtue of a will or received because of an intestacy and the law dictates that they receive the property)

This is a very broad category of independent property and amounts to saying "anything that is in my name now, or during the relationship is going to stay mine."

Exclusion of Interest as a Result of Operation of Law

This wording means that, as general as the foregoing exclusions are, here is a further clarification of how much is being excluded.

5. Without limiting the generality of the foregoing, neither party shall have the right to a division of any independent property, obtain an interest in any independent property, or shall have the right to compensation by reason of any direct or indirect contribution of the party not having an interest, whether by reason of :

a) the use of the Independent Property.

If the couple uses independent property, on their own or as a family, it will not change the status of the property and the other spouse will not acquire an interest in that property. For example, if the family cottage is in the name of the common-law husband, and the family uses it for many years, and the relationship then ends, the cottage will still be excluded from division.

b) circumstances relating to the acquisition, disposition, and preservation,

You will recall that in the cases discussed in Chapter 4, "The Legal Consequences of Living Common Law: Rights and Responsibilities if You Separate," most common-law couples encounter problems at the time of separation because one spouse has invested money or labour in property that is in the name of the other spouse. You will recall Rosa Becker working on the bee farm, and Tracey MacLean working on the cottage property. This clause is stating unequivocally that the financial contribution or labour is not going to result in a spouse acquiring an interest in property that is not in their name.

c) maintenance or improvement of any Independent Property;

d) the parties having disproportionate assets or liabilities; or

This clause makes it clear that the fact that one party has all the property and the other party has all the debt at the end of the relationship will not be a factor in giving a party an interest in property that is classified as independent.

e) the assumption of responsibility for childcare, household management or financial provision;

You will recall again the cases in which one spouse not only worked and contributed their wages to operation of the household budget, but also did all of the childcare and all of the household management. This clause is designed to make sure that each spouse understands that, if they choose to do those things, they will not be acquiring an interest in any of the property in the Independent Property category.

f) any direct or indirect contribution of a party whether or not savings occur through effective management of the household or child rearing responsibilities,

To make it even clearer, this clause states that even if the work that was done or the contribution that was made by the spouse to the effective management of the household or the raising of the children resulted in the other spouse having a greater opportunity to work and build up his or her investment, this will not result in the spouse obtaining an interest in property classified as independent.

g) the use of property for a family purpose,

Again, this clause makes it clear that, even if the family is using the property, it is not going to change its classification from that of Independent Property.

h) any sacrifice made by a party including any sacrifice resulting in loss of career advancement or earning potential; or

This clause makes it abundantly clear that even if the spouse gave up opportunities in their career or passed up opportunities to earn more money, that decision is not going to result in them being compensated with an interest in Independent Property.

i) any economic hardship that a party may suffer as a result of the relationship or its breakdown.

This clause is self-explanatory. It means that no matter how hard the breakdown of the relationship is, it is not going to result in an interest in this property.

Gifts and Dispositions Between the Parties

6. Nothing in this Agreement shall prevent either party from making gifts or testamentary dispositions to the other party.

This clause is designed to ensure that parties can give things to each other without worrying about which category they're going to fall into at a later point should the relationship end. A gift is a gift and it will remain that party's property should the relationship end. This clause also states that testamentary dispositions may be made. This means that common-law spouses may leave gifts to each other in their wills. It also means that just because property was excluded for the purposes of the common-law relationship, does not block one spouse from giving the other spouse a gift. For example, perhaps the family cottage is in the name of the husband alone and is classified as independent property. This cohabitation agreement does not prevent the husband from leaving the family cottage to the common-law wife in his will.

7. Notwithstanding the provision as to making gifts herein, the delivery of property of a value of over One Thousand Dollars ($1,000.00) from one party to the other will be deemed not to be a gift unless evidenced in writing and signed by the party making the gift.

The word "notwithstanding" creates a lot of confusion for people. It really means "even though I said something in the previous sentence, I want to say something more specific right now." The specific term that is being set out here is that "we won't keep track of gifts under $1,000, but if I give you a gift worth more than $1,000, it will need to be in writing and signed by me." This clause means that the following part of the agreement does not override what is set out in other clauses in the agreement.

Division of Property on Separation or Death

8. Except as otherwise specifically provided in this Agreement, if the parties cease to cohabit for a period of ninety days or more or if one party dies, all property, real and personal, acquired during the period the parties cohabit which is not Independent Property shall be divided equally between the parties after having taken into account the income tax consequences of any transfer of interest and assets.

This clause means that the following part of the agreement does not override what is set out in other clauses in the agreement.

The effect of these few words is to say that if we split up for more than 90 days, or if one of us dies, property that doesn't fit into the Independent Property category is going to be divided equally. However, before its value is divided equally, income tax consequences are going to be taken into consideration. For example, if a husband owned a cottage in his name alone, but that cottage was not classified as Independent Property during the relationship and it needed to be transferred to the name of the common-law wife, capital gains tax would be triggered and those taxes would be deducted from the value of the property to be shared equally between the two of them. In this way the income tax consequences of property that is owned equally is not the sole responsibility of just one person. The parties are going to be dividing the net value of their assets equally for assets that do fit in the category of Independent Property.

9. If the parties are unable to agree as to the actual division of the assets, either party may apply to a court of competent jurisdiction for an order allocating specific assets between the parties. If neither party applies for an allocation of assets to a court of competent jurisdiction and the parties are unable to agree on the allocation of assets, the assets shall then be sold and the net proceeds shall be divided equally between the parties forthwith. If the parties are unable to agree on the terms of the listing agreement or of the sale of the asset or assets, either party may apply to a court of competent jurisdiction for the determination of the dispute.

This means, if you can't agree, you are free to ask a court to make a division for you. If you do not want to go to court, but you still cannot agree on how to divide the particular assets, they will be sold and the net proceeds left after the sale will be divided equally between the two people.

If there is real estate involved and the couple needs to sign a listing agreement, but one person will not sign it, then you are off to court again for an order assisting with the sale of the property.

Tracing and Compensation for Benefits

10. If the parties cease to cohabit for a period of ninety days or more, or if one party dies and if either party has converted any Independent Property or any part thereof into other real or personal property that is not Independent Property, the following shall guide the division of property:

This is a very important provision in a cohabitation agreement. It allows a party who has Independent Property to trace that property into other assets. For example, if a party had excluded "all real and personal property inherited by the party" and had $100,000 in cash that they had inherited in an account, and then took the $100,000 of Independent Property and purchased a piece of real estate that did not fit within the category of Independent Property, a method is provided to ensure that the person who had the Independent Property receives a credit for the investment if and when the relationship ends.

a) Before the division referred to herein is effected, the value of the converted property (or the value of the part thereof) shall be traced into the other real or personal property;

Using the example of the $100,000 inheritance and the real property, the value of the inheritance would be traced into the value of the property that was acquired.

b) The party who converted the property shall be reimbursed or given the value of the converted property (or the value of the part thereof);

The inheritance would be credited back to the person who made the investment.

c) The parties shall then share the net equity equally after deducting any liens, charges, or other encumbrances from the market value or sale price at the time.

Once credit has been given for the value of the traced inheritance, anything left over is then divided equally after deduction of liens, charges, or other encumbrances. So, if there is a mortgage on the property, or a contractor had registered a lien, those values are deducted after the inheritance value has been credited back to the other spouse. In this way, the spouse who owns Independent Property will always receive a credit should they move the value of their Independent Property around into various assets. Without this kind of provision, common-law couples with Independent Property would be forced to leave the property frozen in its original form if they wish to protect it.

d) Provided that such tracing shall not occur where the party converting the property specifically elects in writing that the tracing shall not occur with respect to that particular property.

This provision allows the parties to agree that tracing will not occur for a particular piece of property.

SUPPORT

11. The parties acknowledge that they wish to remain completely independent of each other and each will be deemed to be self-supporting and not in need of support from the other. Each of the parties, at all times during the period the parties cohabit, or if they cease to cohabit, is responsible for supporting and maintaining himself or herself.

This is a blanket release of support but the wording is probably inadequate to ensure that the release would be enforced. It certainly captures the intentions of the parties in that it states that they wish to remain completely independent of each other financially, and that they are each self-supporting, but consider the following wording that appears in separation agreements and is considered to be a model clause for spousal support release at the time a couple separates.

Personally, I think that stronger language like the clause below is more likely to be upheld by a court if the parties truly wish to have blanket and complete releases of spousal support.

RELEASE OF SPOUSE SUPPORT

1. As a result of the terms of this agreement, the husband and the wife are financially independent of each other and release his or her rights to spousal support from the other forever. The husband and the wife intend this agreement to be forever final and non-variable.

2. The parties hereby acknowledge that:

(a) This agreement has been negotiated in an unimpeachable fashion and fully represents the intentions and expectations of the parties. Both parties have had independent legal advice and all the disclosure they have asked for and need in order to understand the nature and consequences of this agreement and come to the conclusion, as they do, that the terms of this agreement, including the release of all spousal support rights, constitutes an equitable sharing of both the economic consequences of their relationship and its breakdown.

(b) The provisions of this agreement take into account the overall objectives of the Canadian Law now and in the future and, in particular, take into account the condition, means, needs, and other circumstances of each spouse including the length of time the parties have cohabited, the functions performed by each spouse during the cohabitation, and the other arrangements relating to the support of each spouse. The terms of this agreement

substantially comply with the parties' need to exercise their autonomous rights to achieve certainty and finality.

(c) The terms of this agreement and, in particular, this release of spousal support, reflect their own unique particular objectives and concerns. Among other considerations, they are also depending upon this spousal release, in particular, upon which to base their future lives.

3. The husband and the wife do not want the courts to undermine their autonomy as reflected in the terms of this agreement, which they intend to be a final and certain settling of all issues between them. They wish to have independent lives, no matter what changes may occur. The husband and the wife specifically anticipate that one or both of them may lose their jobs, become ill and be unable to work, have childcare responsibilities that will interfere with their ability to work, find their financial resources diminished or exhausted whether through their own fault or not, or be affected by general economic and family conditions changing over time. Changes in their circumstances may be catastrophic, unanticipated or beyond imagining. Nevertheless, no change, no matter how extreme, will alter this agreement and their view that the terms of this agreement reflect their intention to always be separate financially. The husband and the wife fully accept that no change whatsoever in their circumstances will entitle either of them to spousal support from the other.

4. The parties hereto specifically acknowledge and agree that they have specifically contemplated the meaning of the provisions of Canadian law and that the release of spousal support is not related to the priority for spousal support for which provision is made pursuant to the aforesaid law.

12. Both parties accept the terms hereof in full satisfaction of all claims and causes of action which he or she now has or may hereafter acquire against the other for support.

Support Alternative for Household Expenses

> *The couple can divide responsibility for various expenses including such things as utilities, realty taxes, mortgage payments, credit card debt, or specific expenses related to the operation of the home. If one individual in the relationship wishes to lease a car, their lease payment could be confirmed as being their responsibility. If someone has a health club membership, it can be identified as a specific responsibility of one spouse.*

13. Household and personal expenses shall be dealt with as follows:

a) **Equal Sharing**
The parties shall share equally all costs relating to food, household goods, and furniture and appliance repair.

> *A list of expenses that are to be shared can be set out for complete clarification of obligations during the relationship.*

b) **Joint Bank Account**
The parties shall each pay their share of such costs into a joint bank account to be used by either of them for the purposes set out in this clause.

> *Some couples simply open a joint bank account and deposit their monthly agreed obligation to the account and then cover agreed-upon expenses out of that account by way of automatic deduction.*

c) **Living Expenses**
Each party shall pay for all other living expenses of himself or herself, including his or her own care expense, clothing costs, holiday expense and medical, dental, and prescriptive drug costs.

> *This clause clarifies each party's obligation for their own living expenses and complements paragraph 13 dealing with household expenses. For some couples, being specific is of great assistance to them to avoid arguing over budgets while they cohabit. It is also a valuable way of tracking each person's financial independence through the relationship.*

d) **Children**

___________ will be responsible for those expenses attributable to the his/her children, namely:

Name of child: _________________ Date of Birth: ____________

Name of child: _________________ Date of Birth: ____________

Name of child: _________________ Date of Birth: ____________

> *It may be a good idea to also acknowledge in this section another parent and where that support is allocated in the new family budget.*

e) **Home**

i) ***Ownership***: The lands and premises described in Schedule ____, currently registered in the name of _____________ shall be used as the home of the parties (referred to as the "Home") but shall remain the exclusive Independent Property of ____________.

> *This provision is unequivocal confirmation that a home occupied by the common-law couple shall not be shared in the event of separation or death.*

ii) ***Expenses***: All expenses relating to the Home including, without limiting the generality of the foregoing, the financial encumbrances, taxes, upkeep and maintenance of the Home shall be paid by ______________.

> *"Without limiting the generality of the foregoing" means that some examples are about to be given, but the examples in no way are exhaustive.*

iii) ***Notice to Vacate***: ____________ may give ____________ thirty days' notice to vacate the Home, after which period ________ shall leave ____________ in sole and exclusive occupancy of the Home.

> *This provision allows the owner of the home to give notice to the other common-law spouse if the relationship comes to an end. In addition, it would allow an executor or estate trustee of the estate of a deceased person to give notice to a common-law spouse who continued to reside in the home.*

iv) During the period that ______________ resides in the Home after ______________ has given the notice and up to the time that he/she vacates the Home, ___________ shall not entertain anyone in the Home nor shall he/she change the Home in any way.

*This provision is necessary because it could be unpleasant to have the spouse who is moving out entertaining in the home during the 30-day period or making changes to the home in that 30-day period. It is also possible, of course, to add some wording to this clause that would allow for extensions of the 30-day period by the owner of the property. It is not always possible for someone to find alternative accommodations in a 30-day period**[text box ends]***

f) **Estates**

Subject to the provisions of this Agreement, neither party shall claim any interest in the estate of the other except as specifically provided for by Will or, in the case of an intestacy, as specifically provided for by the laws of the governing jurisdiction relating to the intestate succession.

See the section Rights and Responsibilities If One of You Dies, Is Injured, or Becomes Ill in Chapter 5, "The Legal Consequences of Living Common Law." You will recall from that chapter that the province in which you reside will dictate whether you have any interest in the estate of a deceased common-law spouse. Certainly most provinces allow a surviving common-law spouse to claim support from the estate if he or she were indeed dependent upon the deceased person at the time. However, this provision is designed to block any claim of a surviving common-law spouse unless some provision is contained in the cohabitation agreement.

g) **Testamentary Provisions**

The parties have each made valid Wills naming the other as beneficiary to the extent of $________ and agree not to change their Wills. This provision shall always be a first charge on the Estate of the deceased party.

It is possible for common-law couples to make what are known as "mutual wills." They can also enter into an agreement requiring them to not change their wills after it has been signed. In some cases an actual contract is signed confirming that agreement. However, courts have been willing to enforce mutual wills if there is adequate evidence that the parties had indeed agreed to do so. If a party changes his or her will and therefore violates the agreement, the court may ignore the new will and enforce the previous will against the estate.

This provision allows the surviving common-law spouse who relied upon an agreement for mutual wills to enforce that agreement against the estate of the deceased common-law spouse. In this regard see also paragraph (m) of the cohabitation agreement (below) which makes the cohabitation agreement binding on the heirs, executors, and administrators of a deceased common-law spouse's estate.

h) Care of Children of Former Unions

i) ***Children***: The following children of ______________ and his former relationship shall reside with the parties:

Name of child: ______________ Date of Birth: ______________
Name of child: ______________ Date of Birth: ______________
Name of child: ______________ Date of Birth: ______________

It may be a good idea to set out the actual anticipated residential schedule for the children so that there is no misunderstanding about the potential obligations including not just day-to-day schedules but schooling commitments, major holidays, and summer vacations.

ii) ***Expenses***: All expenses related to the said children, including all expenses for their care and upbringing, shall be the sole responsibility of ______________.

iii) ***Compensation for services***: Where ______________ provides household or childcare services for such children, he/she shall receive reasonable compensation from ___________ for such services within 14 days of the end of the month in which such services were provided. If such compensation is not received, he/she shall receive such compensation within 14 days of delivery of a written calculation of the value of such services to ______________.

This provision is optional. It is unnecessary to provide for such compensation given the provisions of paragraph. 2(c)(iv). However, if compensation for childcare or household services seems appropriate in your particular relationship, this is a useful clause.

iv) If there is a dispute as to the amount of compensation as shown in the written calculation, ___________ shall arbitrate the dispute, and such decision shall be binding upon both parties.
v) If no written calculation and request for compensation is delivered within the 14-day time period stipulated above, there shall be no claim in the future for household or childcare services performed.

i) **Documents**
Without limiting the generality of the foregoing, each party shall do all things necessary to facilitate the fulfillment of the terms of this Agreement by both parties, including providing further information and executing further documents.

This provision is necessary because, at some point in the future, it may be important to have a common-law spouse sign important documents to give effect to the agreement. For example, signing of a listing agreement for a property, signing mortgage documents or transfer documents, tax returns or tax designations related to capital gains, and so on.

j) **Entire Agreement**
This Agreement constitutes the entire agreement between the parties and supersedes all previous communications, representations and agreements, whether verbal or written, between the parties with respect to the subject matter hereof.

This is a very important clause. It confirms that the only agreement is the agreement that is in writing. If the couple has verbal discussions or if they write down even notes to each other, that type of information will not change the interpretation of the cohabitation agreement. The only changes that will be valid are changes that are made in exactly the same way that the agreement was made in the first place—written, signed, and witnessed. In this regard see paragraph (n) below.

k) **Severability**
The invalidity of any particular clause or subclause of this Agreement shall not affect any other clause or subclause of this Agreement, but this Agreement shall be construed as if such invalid clause or subclause were omitted.

This clause allows the cohabitation agreement to be scrutinized and should one clause be considered invalid, it will not wipe out the legal effect of the balance of the agreement. For example, if a couple included a provision that a court considered to affect custody of or access to children, or a provision that eliminated an entitlement to child support, that type of clause could be struck from the cohabitation agreement without affecting the balance of it.

l) **Applicable Law**
This Agreement is made pursuant to the laws of ____________. It shall be interpreted pursuant to the laws of ____________ and the jurisdiction for any adjudication related to this Agreement shall be the ________________ Court (e.g. Ontario). The parties intend this Agreement to be a Cohabitation Agreement in accordance with the provisions of the *Family Law Act*, R.S.O. 1990, c.F.3 , as amended from time to time.

This provision allows you to select the law of a particular province or territory to govern the interpretation of your cohabitation agreement. Even if the couple resides in Manitoba, for example, they could select the law of Ontario to govern their cohabitation agreement.

m) **Heirs and Executors**
This Agreement shall also be binding upon the heirs, executors, and administrators of the parties to this Agreement, who shall do all things necessary for the purpose of carrying out the terms of this Agreement as may then be applicable.

You will recall from Chapter 5, "The Legal Consequences of Living Common Law," that surviving common-law spouses have limited entitlement to claims against the estate. This paragraph confirms that the heirs, executors, estate trustees, and even administrators in the case of an intestacy are bound by the contents of the cohabitation agreement. This means, for example, that Independent Property as set out in the cohabitation agreement will be preserved and will fall into the deceased common-law spouse's estate. That property will be protected in the same way in which it would have been protected had the couple simply separated.

n) Amendments

This Agreement may be amended only by written agreement between the parties with such agreement made in the same way that this Cohabitation Agreement has been made, in writing, signed and witnessed.

o) Legal Advice, Disclosure and Fair Agreement

Each of the parties acknowledges that he or she:

i) has had independent legal advice (insert: as evidenced by the execution of the certificates attached to this agreement);

If one party is not receiving independent legal advice, see the acknowledgment that is at the end of this agreement, whereby a person can acknowledge that they had an opportunity to obtain independent legal advice, but decided not to.

ii) understands the nature and consequences of this Agreement;

See Chapter 9, "Signed, Sealed, and Delivered," with its emphasis on the importance of ensuring that both parties understand exactly what the agreement is attempting to achieve and its effect, both as of the date it is signed and possible implications for the future.

iii) is signing this Agreement voluntarily;

See Chapter 9, "Signed, Sealed, and Delivered," and in particular, those passages on the importance of ensuring that a party is not under duress or undue influence when they sign the agreement.

iv) has made full disclosure to the other of his or her respective significant assets, debts, and liabilities existing at the date of this Agreement as evidenced by the statements contained in Schedules; and

See Chapter 9, "Signed, Sealed, and Delivered," with reference to, the importance of making full financial disclosure, both in terms of assets, debts, and liabilities and the value or extent of those assets, debts, and liabilities.

v) believe that the provisions of this Agreement adequately discharge the present and future responsibilities of the parties to one another and that the contract will not result in circumstances that are unconscionable or unfair to either party (alternate: believes that the provisions of this Agreement are fair).

You will recall that in some cases the court may be prepared to interfere with a cohabitation agreement if the effect of it is unconscionable. This subparagraph is an acknowledgment that the parties consider the agreement to be fair and specifically state that it is not unconscionable or unfair to either of them.

IN WITNESS WHEREOF the parties have hereunto set their hands the day and year first above written:

______________________	______________________
Witness:	By:

____

Name:

____

Address:

____

Occupation:

See Chapter 9, "Signed, Sealed, and Delivered," and, in particular, item 3 of the Three "Must-do's" which explains the proper way to have these agreements witnessed. In particular, it is important to have the witness present at the time the agreement is signed by the party whose signature they are purporting to witness.

CERTIFICATE OF INDEPENDENT LEGAL ADVICE

See Chapter 8, "The Role of Your Lawyer," and Chapter 9, "Signed, Sealed, and Delivered," to understand the significance of obtaining not only independent legal advice, but effective independent legal advice.

I, ______________________, of the ______________________, in the ______________, Lawyer, hereby certify that:

1. I was consulted in my professional capacity by ___________, one of the parties named in the annexed Cohabitation Agreement dated as of _____________, as to his/her rights and obligations under the said Agreement.

2. I acted solely for him/her and explained to him/her the nature and effect of the said Cohabitation Agreement, and he/she acknowledged and declare that the/she fully understood the provisions thereof and it appeared to me that he/she was executing the said Cohabitation Agreement of his/her own volition and without fear, threat, compulsion, or influence by ______________ or any other person.

3. I am subscribing witness to the said Cohabitation Agreement, and I was present and saw it executed by ____________ at___________ on ______________.

DATED at _________ this _________ day of _________, 20___.

____

Name of Lawyer

This acknowledgment can be modified to reflect your actual circumstances. The effect of this acknowledgment is to ensure that a party who has not obtained independent legal advice acknowledges that they had an opportunity to do so. The person who witnesses the signature related to this acknowledgment should be careful to review each paragraph in the acknowledgment with the person who is signing it. In this way it will reduce the likelihood of that acknowledgment being attacked at a later date as having been signed under duress or undue influence.

OR

ACKNOWLEDGMENT OF_______________

1. I, _______________, one of the parties to a Cohabitation Agreement dated the _____ day of _______________, 200_, acknowledge that I was advised by ____(lawyer)____ that he/she could not act for both parties to this Cohabitation Agreement, that he/she represents only my spouse, and that I should seek and obtain independent legal advice before signing this Cohabitation Agreement.

2. Notwithstanding the above, I choose not to seek independent legal advice, and to sign this Cohabitation Agreement not having had the benefit of such advice.

3. I do hereby further decare and acknowledge that:
   a) The said ____(lawyer)____ has not purported to advise me with respect to my rights and obligations under this Cohabitation Agreement;
   b) I have carefully read the provisions of the Cohabitation Agreement and understand the meaning of each and every one of them;
   c) I have signed the Cohabitation Agreement of my own volition, without the pressure of undue influence or coercion of any kind on the part of my spouse or his/her lawyer; and
   d) I do verily believe that the provisions of the Cohabitation Agreement are fair, reasonable, and adequate to protect my interests and those of my spouse.

IN WITNESS WHEREOF I have hereunto set my hand and seal this day of _______________, 20___.

SIGNED, SEALED, AND DELIVERED

in the presence of:

_______________________ _______________________

Witness: By:

____

Name:

~

The foregoing draft cohabitation agreement is designed to assist you in gathering your own thoughts about the possible contents for a cohabitation agreement. Do not hesitate to work with this draft and perhaps consider obtaining some independent legal advice from a lawyer about the way in which the agreement is evolving. You will recall from Chapter 8, “The Role of Your Lawyer,” that it may not be necessary to hire a lawyer for completion of the agreement from start to finish. It is possible to simply buy an hour or two of advice from time to time to make sure you’re on the right track.

Appendices

Appendix A

MY MARRIAGE CONTRACT WORKSHEET—WHAT I OWN AND WHAT I OWE

What do I own?	What is it worth?
1. Real estate	
2. Cottage/recreational property	
3. Vehicles	
4. RRSPs/Savings	
5. Pensions	
6. Stocks and investments	
7. Companies/sole proprietorships	
8. Timeshares	
9. Accounts receivable	
10. Jewellery	
11. Art	
12. Memberships	
13. Sporting equipment	
14. Musical instruments	
15. Furniture	
16. Other property	

What do I owe?	How much and for how long?
1. Mortgages	
2. Line of credit	
3. Credit cards	
4. Taxes	
5. Loans from family	
6. Other loans	
7. Lawsuits	
8. Judgments	
9. Fines	

Appendix B

OUR COHABITATION AGREEMENT SCHEDULES A AND B

SCHEDULE A

Our Cohabitation Agreement Asset and Liability Summary

Asset	Value

Liability	Amount of Liability

SCHEDULE B
Our Cohabitation Agreement Asset and Liability Summary

Asset	Value

Liability	Amount of Liability

Appendix C

SOME CONSIDERATIONS AND KEY DOCUMENT CHECKLIST

A. CONCERNS ABOUT CHILDREN

- Will we have children? Our own? Adoption? How many?
- When would we have children?
- Would one of us stay home from our career?
- What are our attitudes about child rearing?
- What do we each think about religious upbringing?
- Education? Public? Private? Religious?
- Health care? Benefits available?
- Recreation/Sports/Hobbies/Clubs
- Sunset/Termination clauses needed?

B. CONCERNS ABOUT FINANCES

- What are our attitudes about finances?
- What are our debt/assets situations?
- Future liabilities/current savings?
- Taxes owed?
- Future career plans—1 year? 5 years? 10 years?
- Will we buy property? How acquired? Joint account?
- Rent? How will we pay?
- Inheritances now? In future?

- Life insurance?
- Disability insurance?
- Pensions?
- Obligations to previous spouse and children. How much? How long?
- Wills, powers of attorney, letters of intent on joint accounts

C. CONCERNS ABOUT HEALTH

- Significant medical history?
- Family History? Risk? What if one of us gets sick?
- Health risk through employment?
- Mental health history? Concerns?
- Alcohol
- Drugs
- Gambling
- Obsessive-compulsive disorder?
- Mental health history? Concerns?
- Schizophrenia? Bipolar? Manic Depressive?
- Criminal convictions? Pending issues? Record? Pardon?
- Wills, power of attorney for personal care.

D. CONCERNS ABOUT PROPERTY

- How acquired? Contributions?
- How would title be held? Joint. Sole. Tenants-in-common.
- Family property? Inherited?
- Business assets? Inherited? Incorporated.
- Business partners? Working together.
- Maintenance and improvement of each other's property.
- Wills, power of attorney for property.
- When did our cohabitation begin?

DO I HAVE . . .

A Will?

Where is it?
Who is my executor/estate trustee?
Does it need updating?

A Power of Attorney for Personal Care?

Where is it?
Who is the attorney?
Who is the alternate?
Does it need updating?
Does it contemplate instructions for care in the case of emergencies?

A Power of Attorney for Property?

Where is it?
Who is the attorney?
Who is the alternate?
Does it need updating?

Joint Assets/Accounts?

If real estate, where are the documents?
If accounts, what are the account numbers and institutions?
What is our intention with respect to joint assets?
Do I have a letter of intent for joint accounts? Where is it?

Appendix D

TABLE OF COMMON-LAW RIGHTS AND RESPONSIBILITIES

Draft

Province	Common Law Status?	Spousal Support?	Property?	Estate Rights?
B.C.	After 2 years or upon birth of child while cohabiting	Yes/1 year to apply	No statutory rights	May apply to court
Alberta	Yes, but not called common law	Yes—*Adult Interdependent Act*	No statutory rights	No
Saskatchewan*	Treated same as married people	Yes	Yes—statutory rights	Yes
Manitoba*	After 3 years or upon birth of child while cohabiting	Yes	Yes—statutory rights and may register a common-law relationship	Yes
Ontario	After 3 years or upon birth of child while cohabiting	Yes	No statutory rights	No

Province	Common Law Status?	Spousal Support?	Property?	Estate Rights?
Nova Scotia*	After 2 years	Yes	No, but may register a domestic partnership	No
New Brunswick	After 3 years of substantial dependence	Yes	No property rights	No
Newfoundland	After 2 years or upon birth of child while cohabiting	Yes—called a "partner"	No property rights	No
P.E.I.	After 3 years or upon birth of child while cohabiting	Yes	No statutory rights	Yes
N.W.T.*	After 2 years or upon birth of child while cohabiting	Yes	Yes—property rights	Yes
Yukon	Relation-ship of some permanence	3 months to claim	No statutory rights	Yes
Quebec	No common-law rights	None	None	None
Nunavut	After 2 years or upon birth of child while cohabiting	Yes	No statutory rights	Yes

* These provinces and territory have special rules for common-law spouses. For example, in Manitoba and Nova Scotia, there are laws which permit common-law couples to register their relationship and to thereby qualify for extra rights and protections. Check with a family law lawyer in those provinces to discuss the value of registering your relationship in addition to, or instead of, a cohabitation agreement.

In Manitoba see www.gov.mb.ca/justice/family/law or call 1-800-282-8069 ext 3701.

In Nova Scotia see www.gov.ns.ca/just/flic.

Appendix E

CONSENT FOR DISCLOSURE OF CRIMINAL HISTORY INFORMATION

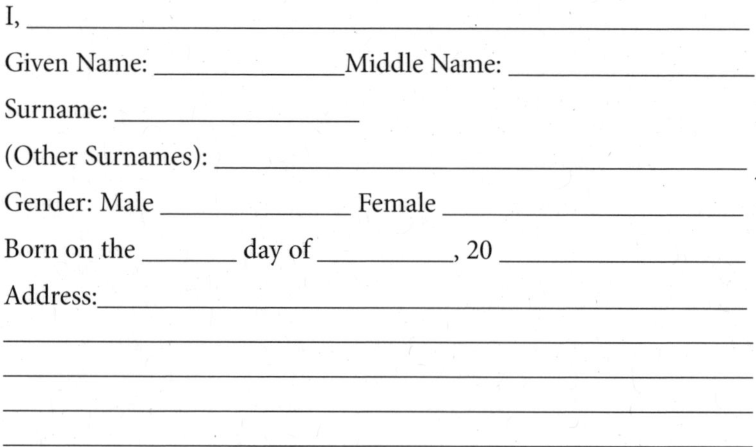

I, ____

Given Name: ______________ Middle Name: ________________

Surname: __________________

(Other Surnames): _________________________________

Gender: Male ______________ Female ________________

Born on the _______ day of __________, 20 ________________

Address: ____

____

____

____

____

having voluntarily provided the above noted personal information, hereby authorize any Canadian Police Agency to conduct a CPIC (Canadian Police Information Centre) search of the "National Repository for Criminal Records in Canada," and any other police information system to which they have access, for criminal information history pertaining to me. I am aware that this search does not include criminal convictions for which a pardon has been granted nor does it include criminal offences that fall under the *Youth Criminal Justice Act (YCJA)*. Therefore, at this time and until I specifically inform you to the contrary in writing, in compliance with all Municipal, Provincial and Federal human rights and privacy legislation, I hereby authorize that the results of this search be released to International Fingerprinting Services Canada (IFSC), who will provide the results directly to:

____

____

____

____

____

____

Signature of Applicant ________________ Date __________________

Appendix F

PERMISSION TO CONDUCT CREDIT REFERENCES

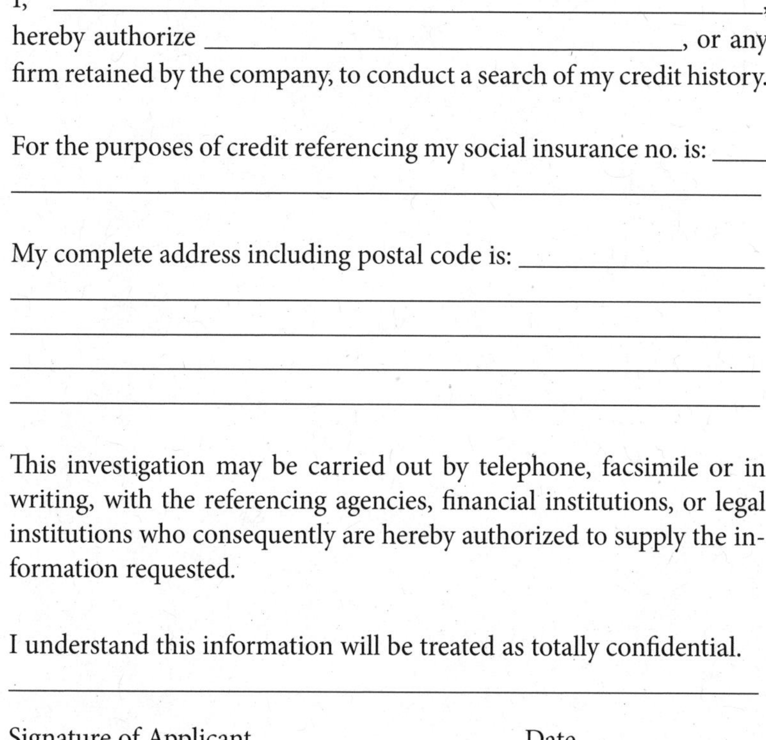

I, ____,
hereby authorize ______________________________, or any firm retained by the company, to conduct a search of my credit history.

For the purposes of credit referencing my social insurance no. is: ____
____

My complete address including postal code is: ________________
____
____
____
____

This investigation may be carried out by telephone, facsimile or in writing, with the referencing agencies, financial institutions, or legal institutions who consequently are hereby authorized to supply the information requested.

I understand this information will be treated as totally confidential.

____

Signature of Applicant ____________________ Date ____________

INDEX

N

O

P

T

U

V

W